CROWD SCENES

D1738797

MICHAEL TRATNER

Crowd Scenes

MOVIES AND MASS POLITICS

FORDHAM UNIVERSITY PRESS
New York / 2008

Library of Congress Cataloging-in-Publication Data

Tratner, Michael.
Crowd scenes : movies and mass politics / Michael Tratner.—1st ed.
   p. cm.
  Includes bibliographical references and index.
  ISBN 978-0-8232–2901–7 (cloth : alk. paper)—ISBN 978–0-8232–2902–4 (pbk. : alk. paper)
  1. Crowds in motion pictures.   2. Motion pictures—Political aspects.
  I. Title.
√PN1995.9.C67T73   2008
  791.45'6552—dc22   2008005864

Printed in the United States of America
10 09 08   5 4 3 2 1
First edition

CONTENTS

ACKNOWLEDGMENTS

*T*his book extends and responds to the themes and issues explored in my first book, *Modernism and Mass Politics: Joyce, Woolf, Eliot, Yeats.* In switching the focus of my research from difficult literary texts to movies, I am building on the work of many colleagues such as R. Brandon Kershner, Pamela Caughie, Colin MacCabe, James Morrison, and Jennifer Wicke who have led the way in exploring the common cultural roots of modernist and popular texts. I also owe much to Bryn Mawr College and my colleagues in the English Department and the Film Studies Program for creating an intellectual environment that encourages faculty to develop new realms of expertise in teaching and research. I am indebted to Lesley Brill and Katherine Rowe for their generous criticism and advice, and to Ray Scott for creating the cover art. The continued editorial support of Helen Tartar has been invaluable. And finally I wish to thank Leda Sportolari, Jeffrey Tratner, and Cara Tratner for years of provocative discussions of movies.

CROWD SCENES

INTRODUCTION:
MOVIES AND THE HISTORY
OF CROWD PSYCHOLOGY

*T*he movies and the masses erupted on the world stage together: in a few short decades around the turn of the twentieth century, millions of people who rarely could afford a night at the theater and who had never voted in an election became regular paying customers at movie palaces and proud members of brand new political parties. The question of how to represent the masses fascinated and plagued politicians and filmmakers, who struggled in their different ways to express the dreams of the new audiences. There was a sense of great promise: movies were hailed as the universal language and mass participation in politics was hailed as the precursor to fabulous new social orders, dissolving class and national boundaries.

For some, however, the dream of a new age seemed more a nightmare. The most influential prophet of the new era, Gustave Le Bon, warned of the end of recognizable civilization: "While all our ancient beliefs are tottering and disappearing, while the old pillars of society are giving way one by one, the power of the crowd is the only force that nothing menaces, and of which the prestige is continually on the increase. The age we are about to enter will be in truth the Era of Crowds."[1] Le Bon called on governments to change the way they reached their constituents, to adopt new methods of speaking and governing in order to reach the crowd. During the twenties, he declared that the movies were the ideal medium for reaching the crowd and "urged government ownership of cinema theaters" and government control of

1

filmmaking.[2] Several governments agreed and set up ministries of movies, but not the capitalist governments Le Bon hoped to preserve. Rather, governmental control of the movie industry became a cornerstone of the new political movements which embraced the crowd as the ideal basis of the social order: communist and fascist regimes. Political theorists in such regimes often cited Le Bon's belief that the masses and the movies had a natural attraction to each other, and drew the conclusion that movies inherently supported collectivist, anti-individualist, and anticapitalist politics.

Needless to say, Hollywood filmmakers were rendered quite uncomfortable by such conclusions, but they did not simply deny that movies had any inherent attraction to mass politics. Rather, Hollywood believed that it was possible to control that attraction and passed industry regulations requiring movies to be constructed so as to limit and channel the power of crowd psychology—and to counter the efforts of filmmakers in collectivist countries. If we examine the representations of masses—the crowd scenes—in Hollywood films and contrast them with such scenes in communist and fascist films, we discover what could be called a political debate carried out in elements of filmic style. In this book I am going to trace the contours of that debate; the analysis establishes the crucial importance of crowd scenes to the ideological structure of movies during the twentieth century. Crowd scenes are not merely backgrounds for stories; they also function as models for the crowd in the theater, and as such they reveal the ways filmmakers conceive of and hope to control the moviegoing experience.

Film criticism has largely ignored crowd scenes and crowd reactions of audiences. Indeed, the highly influential work of film theorists such as Christian Metz, Kaja Silverman, and Laura Mulvey essentially denies that there are any crowd emotions in the reactions to Hollywood films, treating the audience as a collection of separate individuals, "spectators" who sit in the dark and have one-to-one fantasy relationships with the characters on the screen. Such theorists describe the audience as if it were just one person, speaking in the singular of "the Male Gaze," the "All-Perceiving Subject," the "Voyeur," and "The Spectator," never of crowd responses or mass fantasies or social trends.

Hollywood filmmakers and those who track the industry, on the other hand, have thought and written quite a bit about crowd responses, mass fantasies, and social trends, particularly the trends that lead massive numbers of people to stand in long lines outside theaters. It makes sense that Hollywood movies would be constructed to create and regulate such crowd responses. One of the main ways to shape mass reactions is to show on the screen masses reacting: not surprisingly, the most popular movies have always been full of immense crowd shots, from *The Birth of a Nation* through *Gone with the Wind* to *Titanic*. It may seem strange in the largely postcommunist and postfascist world to imagine that film-makers worried that such crowd scenes were fraught with political dangers. Public discourse about major world conflicts no longer focuses much attention on contrasts between individualism and crowd politics. But throughout the first half of the twentieth century there was an often-repeated fear that any crowd that began thinking about politics was in danger of turning into a mob espousing anti-individualist politics. The fear that all movies tend toward nondemocratic mass politics peaked of course in the 1950s blacklist, where Hollywood filmmakers were accused of having slipped communist propaganda into a remarkable range of films. The effectiveness of such accusations on the film industry has never been fully explained; the House Un-American Activities Committee (HUAC) accused nearly every industry in America of being full of communists, but only in Hollywood did these accusations cause mass firings. I suggest that part of the effectiveness of the HUAC in Hollywood derived from the fact that filmmakers themselves had always feared that their movies had a natural attraction to un-American politics, regardless of how thoroughly the stories presented were pro-American.

Such fears appeared long before the HUAC hearings. In 1919, for example, guidelines of the Committee on Public Information, reprinted in the *New York Times*, cautioned against pictures containing "mob scenes and riots which might be entirely innocent in themselves but [could be] distorted and used adversely to the interests of the U.S."[3] The committee not only feared that the United States might appear badly if the world knew about riots in the country, but also—believing the spirit of riots antithetical to U.S. ideology—feared the political consequences of the representation of riots within movies. In the 1920s, the American Committee of the Motion Picture Industry of the United States found it necessary to declare itself devoted to combating "Bolshevism, radicalism and revolutionary sentiment" in movies.[4] The need for such committees suggests that it was considered difficult to tell when such ideas would creep into films.

Hollywood's concern about the crowd effects of movies is most powerfully expressed in the Movie Production Code of 1930, the infamous Hays Code. The Code has become most well known for requiring married couples to never be seen in the same bed, but it does not develop its call for censorship from concerns about sexuality. Rather, it develops its argument for the need for censorship by presenting a theory of the natural relationship between movies and the newly active masses appearing throughout the world. The Code begins by outlining a vision of that relationship: "Most arts appeal to the mature. This art appeals at once to every class—mature, immature, developed, undeveloped, law-abiding, criminal. Music has its grades for different classes; so has literature and drama. This art of the motion picture, combining as it does the two fundamental appeals of looking at a picture and listening to a story, at once reaches every class of society."[5]

The description, though it repeats the word "class" over and over again, might nonetheless seem rather apolitical, expressing only a worry about the effect of movies on the "immature" and deviants. However, Steven J. Ross's archival work shows that when the Code was put into effect, "censors found films dealing with class struggle even more threatening than cinematic displays of sex and violence."[6] We might then say that the Code has "coded" concerns about the lower classes as concerns about criminality, immaturity, and underdevelopment. Such a definition of what makes a class "lower" serves well to suggest that what many feared was a coming struggle between the masses and the old ruling classes was really nothing more than the struggle of the immature and deviant against the decent.

If the writers of the Code were really worried about "immature" viewers, we might wonder why they did not simply embrace what the movie industry came to much later—a system of regulating who is allowed into which movies, keeping the immature viewers out of movies with mature themes. The problem with such an idea in 1930 was that the difference between the immature and the mature, the undeveloped and the developed, was not seen simply as a difference in age, but rather as a difference that resided inside everyone: everyone had "immature" or "lower" qualities which movies had the power to bring out. Furthermore, this lowering effect of movies was believed to derive precisely from the broad appeal of movies. As the Hays Code puts it, "Psychologically, the larger the audience the lower the moral mass resistance to suggestion."[7] "Moral mass resistance to suggestion" is a peculiar, possibly incoherent notion, which might seem to allude to something that would stop a crowd from turning into a mob. The Code, though, does not discuss the dangers of people leaving movie theaters in wild-eyed gangs, but rather connects this "lowering" effect to the wide distribution of movies across the country, simultaneously reaching quite varied audiences. The Code implies that because such varied kinds of people face

4

the same suggestions all at once, the "moral mass resistance to suggestion" of the entire nation is lowered. Movies seemed capable of altering the psychology of those watching, so that they no longer had "individual" personalities but rather joined together in a "crowd mind" that was inherently "lower" in morality and unable to resist suggestions.

Sociologists specializing in crowd psychology joined in tracing the connection between movie viewing and the loss of individual self-control. For example, Herbert Blumer, professor of sociology at the University of Chicago and president of the American Sociological Association, wrote in the 1930s that movies "arrest attention, check intrusion, and acquire control. The individual loses himself in the picture," with the result that the audience watching a movie ends up having "certain features of the mob."[8]

Recent work in film history has started to examine the history of actual audience behavior, and found that the scene of movie watching in the first few decades may have contributed to the sense of the movie audience as a mob. Thomas Doherty, after reading numerous accounts of audience responses, summarizes the scene of 1930s movie watching: "Congregated together in crowds of hundreds, and sometimes thousands, audiences reacted in a group unity that was garrulous and demonstrative, sometimes boorish and unruly, often communal and choral."[9] Vanessa Schwartz's study of turn-of-the-century cinema leads her to conclude that people went to movies at first as an outgrowth of other public gatherings and spectacles, and being part of a crowd was part of the reason for being there. She concludes, "It is necessarily among a crowd that we find the cinematic spectator."[10] Such research supports critics who have begun examining ways crowds are portrayed within movies; Lesley Brill, for example, has drawn on Elias Canetti's political theories to write the first full critical examination of crowds, a superb treatise showing that crowds in Hollywood movies are deeply enmeshed with complex notions of power.[11]

The relationship of movies to crowds was touched on by a few film critics before Brill, though the topic has generally remained peripheral to film analysis. For example, Stanley Cavell quite casually declares that there has always been an inherent relationship between movies and mass politics in his 1971 book, *The World Viewed*. After noting first that Hollywood movie plots have "an inherent tendency toward the democratic," Cavell adds a parenthetical caveat: "(But because of film's equally natural attraction to crowds, it has opposite tendencies toward the fascistic or populistic.)"[12] Another term for the fascistic or populistic political philosophies is "collectivist," so that what Cavell is suggesting is that film has a "natural attraction" to collectivism. To Cavell, this is so obvious that it can be added as a parenthetical aside.

One film critic has drawn considerable attention to the relationship between movies and the new mass movements of the twentieth century: Siegfried Kracauer, who began his career in Weimar as Nazism emerged and then fled to Hollywood. Kracauer summarized what he viewed as the obvious historical connection between film and the masses in his 1960 *Theory of Film*: "Masses of people in the modern sense entered the historical scene only in the wake of the industrial revolution. Then they became a social force of first magnitude . . . The traditional arts proved unable to encompass and render [them] . . . Only film . . . was equal to the task of capturing them in motion. In this case the instrument of reproduction came into being almost simultaneously with one of its main subjects. Hence the attraction which masses exerted on still and motion picture cameras from the outset. . . . D. W. Griffith . . . showed how masses can be represented cinematically. The Russians absorbed his lesson, applying it in ways of their own."[13]

When Kracauer notes that the Russians developed "ways of their own" for using what early Hollywood filmmakers discovered—the power of images of crowds—he suggests the contrast I wish to explore: the Soviets celebrated the power of films to transform audiences into political crowds, while Hollywood turned soon after Griffith to censoring that power out of their films. The Russians were quite direct in claiming this goal: Sergei Eisenstein stated as his credo that his films would be built on the principle of "discarding the individualist conception of the bourgeois hero" and instead "insisting on an understanding of the mass as hero."[14] The valuing of crowd emotions over individual consciousness runs throughout communist and fascist political commentary: Marx called for a return to the "ecstasies" and "enthusiasm" of "riots" as far preferable to the "icy water of egotistical calculation."[15]

Hitler is even more direct in *Mein Kampf* about the value of the riotous emotions which a crowd is believed to generate. He says that the goal of his closely orchestrated "mass demonstrations" is to cause each person to be "swept away . . . into the mighty effect of suggestive intoxication and enthusiasm, . . . the magic influence of what we designate as 'mass suggestion.'"[16]

Note the similarity of the conceptions which are invoked by Hitler to those invoked by the Hays Code: Hitler praises the "magic influence of mass suggestion" and designs his mass rallies to create it; the Hays Code fears the "lower . . . moral mass resistance to suggestion" produced by

6

large audiences at movies, and forces moviemakers to design films to avoid the political dangers of such effects. The similarity between what movies seemed to do to people and what mass demonstrations and riots seemed to do was noted by numerous writers in the early twentieth century; as the film historian Jane Gaines comments, "One can't help noticing the way motion pictures have been closely aligned with and even analogized with riots, particularly during the early decades of cinema."[17] The relationship between movies and riots slid easily into a fear that movies could have political consequences unintended by moviemakers.

The Hays Code was designed to reduce such unintended consequences—but not to entirely eliminate them, because it was not considered possible for film viewers to escape crowd psychology. Contrary to what film theorists claim, Hollywood filmmakers and early-twentieth-century sociologists never believed that audiences would react as isolated individuals. Hollywood moguls concluded that the only way to keep the crowd psychology elicited by movies from tearing the American democratic society apart was by controlling the kinds of suggestions which are made when people's moral mass resistance is lower. Suggestions could be given for people to support democratic institutions. In other words, while unable to think as individuals, people could be given strong motivation to believe that the best way for society to operate is for people to act as individuals. The power of crowd psychology is used, in effect, to counter that very power. As we will see, this produces the paradoxical effect that Hollywood movies contain elements that can be seen as functioning to warn people against the power of movies themselves. The Hays Code in a sense requires movies to serve this function, to be constructed so as to minimize dangers that are inherent in the medium. Hollywood films seek to shape the crowd reactions they stimulate, aiming at a form of "collective spectatorship" rather different from what has been postulated in "spectator theory," as I will show in Chapter 1.

One of Hollywood's main strategies for channeling the power of crowd emotions created by movies can be seen in the strange way that the Hays Code switches topics in the middle of its discussion: after describing crowd psychology for several pages, the Code switches its focus to ways individuals act in private, particularly to sexual and criminal acts. The dangers of the lowering of "mass resistance" are not seen in mass behavior at all, but rather in alterations in individuals' private lives. This shift is set up in those opening lines I quoted earlier, in which "class" seems to be defined in terms of the behavior of individuals (as mature or immature, criminal or law-abiding) rather than in terms of economics. The shift from concern about masses or classes to concern about private lives is central to Hollywood's answer to the appeal of crowd politics: Hollywood movies repeatedly imply that the passions driving crowds are actually desires to have certain kinds of private lives. Crowd emotions function to set up the conditions for satisfying private relationships. We might say then that in Hollywood movies, crowd politics is misguided sexuality. Such a notion is not merely a Hollywood invention; for example, Walter Lippmann, one of the most influential political commentators and a strong defender of individualism in the 1920s, writes that even trying to think about society as a collective whole will result in unleashing wildly dangerous emotions. "To aim at justice among the interests of individuals," he writes, "is to keep opinion wholesome by keeping it close to intelligible issues: to aim at a purposeful collectivism is to go off into the empty air and encourage a collective madness in which, for want of rational criteria, the darkest and most primitive lusts are churned up."[18] Lippmann's words parallel one of the ways Hollywood has sought to solve the problem of the collectivist tendency of movies: by characterizing the difference between individualism and collectivism as the difference between wholesomeness and lust, Lippmann slips from the language of politics into the language of sexuality. The Hays Code makes a similar move, starting off speaking of the dangers of class differences and collective emotions and then shifting to speaking about sexuality and criminality. The shift from sociopolitical to sexual language in the Hays Code and in Walter Lippmann's account is not simply a way of ignoring the political issues which hover around the notion of collective passions. Rather, it is an important method developed in the twentieth century by noncollectivist nations such as the United States to redirect the powerful emotions generated by crowds. In response to the claims of collectivist writers such as Marx and Hitler that mass meetings, crowd experiences, and even riots generate important political emotions, individualists argued that the intense emotions which emerge in crowds are all sexual in nature. If that is so, then crowd scenes can be used as powerful stimulants in movies, so long as the emotions churned up are properly directed into the bedroom—or into institutions which support private relationships.

Sigmund Freud is of course the main source for the belief that crowd emotions are sexual, and he provides an even more dramatic statement than Lippmann or the Hays Code of what happens when large numbers of persons share the same experience: "when it becomes a question of a large number of people, not to say millions, all individual moral acquisitions are obliterated and only the most primitive, the oldest, the crudest

8

mental attitudes are left."[19] Freud proposes an antidote to this crowd effect: overt sexuality. In 1920, in *Group Psychology and the Analysis of the Ego*, he says that "directly sexual impulses . . . disintegrate every group formation."[20] He also says that this effect depends on the historically modern form of heterosexual romance, not just on sexuality: "the opposition between sexual love and group ties is . . . a late development." What Freud calls "earlier" forms of sexuality (including homosexuality) do not work to dissolve group ties; they are compatible with the herd.[21] Freud concludes that the modern form of "love for women breaks through the group ties of race, of national divisions, and of the social class system, and it thus produces important effects as a factor in civilization." As Freud puts it, two people declaring they are in love "are making a demonstration against the herd instinct, the group feeling."[22]

Freud implies that love stories can be used to counter collectivism, and Hollywood movies have followed his lead, but not simply by treating love as the antidote to the herd instinct, because, as we have seen in the Hays Code, Hollywood does not believe that the herd instinct can be eliminated from the moviegoing experience. Hollywood has instead sought to channel the herd emotions into dreams of love. Indeed, we might say that Hollywood has found what Lippman called the "lusts . . . churned up" by crowds pursuing political goals to be quite useful. D. W. Griffith developed this structure in the most popular movie of the first two decades of the twentieth century, *The Birth of a Nation*, as I will show in Chapter 2. Following Griffith's lead, all the later most popular love stories—*Gone with the Wind*, *The Sound of Music*, *Titanic*, and *Doctor Zhivago*[23]—place their central passions against backdrops of huge crowds pursuing political ends or raising political issues. (*Titanic* might not seem to fit this model, but its love story is set against a backdrop of class conflict; its director James Cameron even described the movie as "holding just short of Marxist dogma."[24]) We could also include in this list the movie often called the most popular, though it did not really sell that well, *Casablanca*. Critics have focused nearly all their attention in discussing these films on the characters and the love stories, generally treating the mass political events surrounding the love affairs as background or contrast. But I will show in Chapter 3 that if we examine these movies carefully, we see that the political passions parallel and facilitate the love affairs. The madness of the political crowds in these movies do not stand in the way of sexual passions; they release those passions. Scarlett needs the Civil War to kill her husbands and force her into Rhett's arms, as Zhivago and Laura need the Russian Revolution to remove them from their marriages and thrust them together. The psychoanalytic psychology which has most often been used by film theorists would treat the parallels of sexual and political stories in these movies as evidence that politics is fueled by misplaced sexuality. I propose that these movies are based on exactly the opposite notion, on a perhaps accidental discovery by moviemakers that the most powerful and romantic sexual desires can emerge out of moments of mass political passion. As we will see in Chapter 3, Hollywood has introduced a feeling of permanent political revolution into the structure of modern love.

Hollywood's use of sexuality to redirect the political effects of the crowd was, of course, resisted by collectivist filmmakers. Instead of implying that private passions are the only true emotions, collectivist filmmakers show that public passions are the highest development of private passions, the culmination of feelings generated in private relationships. Collectivist filmmakers end up creating what can be called public forms of sexuality and gender, surprising alternatives to the more familiar notions of sexuality and gender in Hollywood films, as I will show in Chapter 4.

To end this book, I turn to one filmmaker, Fritz Lang, who was highly successful in both protofascist Weimar and in Hollywood. Lang's movies acutely register the difference between Hollywood and "collectivist" film styles, but not because he was a passive recipient of whatever sociopolitical milieu surrounded him, but rather because he was acutely in touch with that central element of the political debates surrounding the two styles: the mysterious power of crowds to transform the minds of individuals who enter them. Lang's movies throughout his life show mass public passions in all their chaotic power, and then generally explore the failure of various systems for controlling such passions. His career put him in the center of the debate between fascist and Hollywood filmmaking: His early German films were considered pro-Nazi films, particularly because the screenwriter on those films, his wife Thea Von Harbou, supported Hitler and remained in Germany to make films for the Nazi party when Lang came to America. Lang denounced Von Harbou and emphatically denied Nazi influence on his early films. Finally, after Von Harbou died, Lang returned to Germany to remake two of his early films. These last remakes are strangely autobiographical: they can be read as efforts to explain how he and his films were caught up (or we might say seduced) into the spirit of Nazism. They are undoubtedly self-serving, but they are fascinating nonetheless as Lang's efforts to bridge the opposed styles of fascist and Hollywood films, and suggest the disturbing conclusion that actually the styles—and the politics associated with them—are not really so opposed.

The notions of crowd psychology which shaped the practices of all the moviemakers discussed in this book may in fact be utterly false. Recent studies have suggested that crowds do not become mobs very easily at all, and that individuals do not really "lose themselves" or change their moralities or their politics much when they become parts of crowds. However, what one recent history called "the myth of the madding crowd" has been remarkably consistent and strong during the last century, and has played a very large role in the history of movies.[25] That this belief of filmmakers has been largely ignored by critics could seem surprising, but perhaps the reason critics have done so is the result of another historical conception which has shaped the way nearly all critics of aesthetic objects (films, literature, painting, music) have done their work: the conception that artists and their proper audiences are individuals who do not themselves lose their heads when creating, viewing, or commenting upon art. It is intriguing to see that historically filmmakers did not think such was the case. Hollywood films imply that before individual personalities can function to control emotions and behaviors—before individual personalities can even be visible—social structures have to be in place to block or channel the power of crowds. Collectivist films imply that to view their works at all requires dropping the individual perspective and joining the crowd. It may be possible, then, to see in Hollywood and in collectivist movies a challenge to some basic assumptions of recent literary and film criticism. By examining how filmmakers have used conceptions of mass consciousness, we may gain not only a better understanding of movies as historical products involved in political debates, but also an understanding of some of the historical limitations which continue to shape the practice of criticism today.

1

COLLECTIVE
SPECTATORSHIP

*I*n the 1970s and '80s, film theorists developed "spectator theory," claiming to have found complex structures that underlie the movie-going experience, then showing that these structures were manipulated by filmmakers (perhaps without fully understanding them) to promote ideological purposes. Moviegoers, sitting in the dark, watching emotionally provocative scenes, became receptive to effects that played on deep psychoanalytic structures to turn everyone into a single unified model of a "spectator." Recently, critics such as Mary Anne Doane and Manthia Diawara have expanded spectator theory to theorize how people who do not fit the prescribed definition of a spectator work out ways of viewing movies.[1] Miriam Hansen, in *Babel and Babylon: Spectatorship in American Silent Film,* has further complicated the theory by tracing the way that the unified model of a single type of spectator emerged from earlier models of multiple cultural groups all viewing movies in different ways and developing their own film industries.[2]

In all these critical accounts, Hollywood filmmakers seem to be trying above all to unify audiences, but I have found that, throughout history, a unified audience deeply troubled filmmakers—and politicians. It was precisely a fear of what might be unleashed if everyone in a vast nation responded with the same emotions that led to Hollywood's censorship of its own movies, codified in the Movie Production Code of 1930. The Code justifies censorship entirely in terms of a nonpsychoanalytic theory of crowd psychology—more a fear than a theory—that when large, varied audiences all experience the same emotions, there is a general lowering of "mass moral resistance to suggestion."

The fear of the power of movies to produce mass suggestions led to distinctive structures within Hollywood movies—while the desire to *promote* mass suggestions led to different structures within communist and fascist movies. If we bring together an account of filmmakers' nonpsychoanalytic theory of crowd psychology with an analysis of the movie structures that manipulated that psychology, we can extract a theory of "collective spectatorship." To see how Hollywood's portrayals of crowds operate as a form of spectatorship, it will be useful to begin by first outlining the basic elements of the more familiar spectator theory.

Roughly, the theory, created in the 1970s, has three elements: a psychological theory; a description of the "cinematic apparatus," the structure of movie projection; and an analysis of the distinctive style of Hollywood movies. In spectator theory, the psychological theory is psychoanalysis. The apparatus is described as comprising "the darkness of the auditorium, the resultant isolation of the individual spectator, the placement of the projector, source of the image behind the spectator's head."[3] This structure makes movie watching rather like dreaming in bed in the dark. The stylistic features of movies noted by spectator theorists are mostly those which produce the effect that the movie world is a complete, sealed reality, plus those which define geometrically and socially a position from which the movie is supposed to be viewed, a position which Nick Browne calls the "spectator-in-the-text."[4] The viewer thus seems both completely removed from the film world and located in a distinct position, becoming, as Miriam Hansen puts it, "the transcendental vanishing point of specific spatial, perceptual, social arrangements."[5] The sense that there is a transcendental point from which to view everything draws on unconscious feelings from early childhood that end up fueling ideological effects: the feelings everyone had for seemingly godlike parents are transferred to the dominant group within society, and the viewer is projected as an ideal member of this dominant group (in the United States, white middle-class males).

To construct an alternative theory of collective spectatorship, then, we need versions of the same three elements: 1) an alternative, nonpsychoanalytic psychology; 2) an alternative description of the cinematic apparatus; and 3) an alternative list of features of movies which elicit the crowd response rather than turning viewers into isolated spectators. All these necessary elements can be found in the Motion Picture Production Code of 1930, dubbed the Hays Code after Will H. Hays, the head of the organization that wrote it. The Hays Code starts by declaring that movies are "entertainment" of a peculiar kind, which produces strange effects never encountered in any entertainment before, effects which so powerfully threaten to compromise moviegoers' morality that movie-makers must censor themselves. The Code says these effects are produced by the ways movies reach audiences, in other words by the "cinematic apparatus." That apparatus in the Hays Code, however, is quite unlike that found in spectator theory:

> A) Most arts appeal to the mature. This art appeals at once to every class—mature, immature, developed, undeveloped, law-abiding, criminal. Music has its grades for different classes; so has literature and drama. This art of the motion picture, combining as it does the two fundamental appeals of looking at a picture and listening to a story, at once reaches every class of society.
>
> B) Because of the mobility of a film and the ease of picture distribution, and because of the possibility of duplicating positives in large quantity, this art reaches places unpenetrated by other forms of art.
>
> C) Because of these two facts, it is difficult to produce films intended for only *certain classes of people*. The exhibitor's theatres are for the masses, for the cultivated and the rude, mature and imma-ture, self-restrained and inflammatory, young and old, law-respect-ing and criminal.[6]

Instead of focusing on the darkness and supposed isolation of audience members, as spectator theory does, the Hays Code describes screenings in terms of the broad distribution of prints and the resultant large audiences. Movies have more "mobility" than any other art form and as a result reach quite varied audiences. The Code thus seems to disagree with the '70s spectator theory which says that Hollywood movies are constructed by projecting an audience of persons completely identical to each other (to be more precise, spectator theory says that movies set up a response that lets each person abstract from his or her position in society into an identically transcendent position). The two theories, however, are not simply contradictory: Miriam Hansen has argued that historically, the "spectator" structure developed precisely as a way to overcome the mixed character of movie audiences, "to stabilize . . . contradictions" and to impose a sense of uniformity of response on quite varied movie-goers.[7] What the Hays Code shows, however, is that it took much more to deal with the variations within movie audiences than just structuring each movie to imply a transcendent, and hence identical, white middle-class male spectator.

14

The problem with large varied audiences is that people within them are no longer individuals, and so cannot assume the role of ideal spectator. The Code invokes a theory of crowd psychology to explain this problem, which it summarizes in one sentence: "Psychologically, the larger the audience the lower the moral mass resistance to suggestion."[8] The sentence seems to invoke commonplace notions of mob psychology and riots, in which people gathered together succumb to "suggestion" and lose control of themselves, lose their "moral resistance." But in conjunction with the description of the cinematic apparatus—movies shown all over the country to different kinds of audiences—the invocation of crowd psychology draws attention to a variation of the problem of mobs: it points to a belief in what happens when people all over the country in many different venues are given the same stimulation, the same suggestion.

The concern about certain images or ideas appearing all over a large society is much older than the Hays Code. One of the best descriptions of this effect was written by John Stuart Mill in 1859, long before movies, yet his description fits the way movies operate remarkably well. He wrote his famous essay, *On Liberty*, in order to counter what he calls a "social tyranny more formidable than many kinds of political oppression . . . the tyranny of the prevailing opinion and feeling . . . the tendency of society, by other means than civil penalties, to impose its own ideas . . . to fetter the development, and, if possible, prevent the formation of any individuality not in harmony with its ways."[9] Far more than people becoming suggestible to widespread opinions and feelings, Mill fears the destruction of individuality. Mill goes on to provide an explanation of how "prevailing opinion and feeling" destroys individuality: through the "magical influence of custom, which is not only, as the proverb says, a second nature, but is continually mistaken for the first," which leads to "enslaving the soul itself."[10] In other words, it is not simply "ideas" commonly held by millions that produce this magical effect, but a set of images of what is "natural," a "second nature" which is mistaken for the "first." Mill shows that long before movies came along people worried about the effects of false images of the real, or in other words, ideological effects. The Hays Code too worries about the ways people mistake images for reality; it speaks of the vividness of movie images and their ability to bring stories "closer" to audiences than plays ever could, giving movies "the apparent reality of life."[11]

Speaking of the vividness and easy readability of movies brings us to the third element necessary to construct crowd response theory: a set of

15

stylistic or "textual" features of movies which are believed to elicit the responses that are described as occurring in audiences. The realism of Hollywood movies is one of the central tenets of spectator theory, and the Hays Code suggests that realism also functions to produce crowd responses. The Code goes on, however, to focus on certain elements overlooked by spectator theory, in particular a list of three that are credited with special power in moving audiences: "The grandeur of mass meetings, large action, spectacular features, etc., affects and arouses more intensely the emotional side of the audience."[12] To arouse the emotional side is to draw people away from their rational or moral sides, so what the Hays Code is saying is that these three elements of movies are particularly effective at lowering the moral mass resistance of audiences.

The first term in the list—the "grandeur of mass meetings"—seems a very odd thing for the Code to mention, since it is difficult to think of any Hollywood movies that show mass meetings at all, much less ones creating a sense of grandeur. What comes to mind when one thinks of movies showing the grandeur of mass meetings are Leni Riefenstahl's film *Triumph of the Will* and Sergei Eisenstein's *The Battleship Potemkin*. I do not think it is a mistake to bring up such movies: the concern about crowds in Hollywood movies during the classical era was in part a concern about the politics of mass movements, and in particular an effort to protect the United States against the political systems based on mass movements rather than on individual voting—communist and fascist systems. Communist and fascist leaders agreed with the Hays Code that large audiences make people suggestible, but they thought this was a wonderful effect that promotes morality. The ministries of propaganda in fascist and communist countries actively promoted films full of scenes of grand mass gatherings.

I will discuss fascist and communist films in Chapter 4; for now, it is enough to note the oddity of the phrase, "grandeur of mass meetings," and to consider why it gets placed as an equal to "large action" and "spectacular features". The list suggests that mass meetings, large action, and spectacular features share a certain quality, and it is not hard to see what might be underlying this trio of filmic features: all of them carry viewers away from the world of friends and families into scenes too big to be experienced intimately; the Code implies that filmmakers believed such scenes would generate the psychological responses of people as part of a mass.

These three types of scenes all would be presented in long shots, and long shots function for crowd response theory the way that point-of-view shots and the shot/reverse shot structure function for spectator theory: point-of-view shots define the position spatially and emotionally from which the projected spectator is to view everything; similarly long shots create what could be called the "crowd-in-the-text" by defining the position spatially and emotionally from which the projected large audience described in the Hays Code is to view everything. Adapting a term from Louis Althusser, we can say that long shots and in particular crowd shots "interpellate" the large audience directly, creating an image of the kind of crowd that is observing the movie and implying that the crowd should have certain qualities and not other qualities.[13] Movies "hail" their audiences as crowds in ways parallel to but distinct from the ways they hail audience members as individuals.

One other feature of movies is highlighted in the Code as of particular power in conveying suggestions into audiences, namely stars:

> The enthusiasm for and interest in the film *actors* and *actresses*, developed beyond anything of the sort in history, makes the audience largely sympathetic toward the characters they portray and the stories in which they figure. Hence they are more ready to confuse the actor and character, and they are most receptive of the emotions and ideals portrayed and presented by their favorite stars.[14]

Stars are not exactly "textual" features of movies; rather, as the Code notes, they exist partly within and partly outside of movies, and one crucial part of their power is that they cause audiences "to confuse the actor and character." Psychoanalytic spectator theory, for all its concern about who is looking at what, pays little attention to the strange position of stars as only partly contained within Hollywood movies. For one thing, spectator theory postulates that everything is done by Hollywood movies to make people forget they are watching a movie—the diegetic world is supposedly experienced as a sealed reality. Stars break up that sealed reality by bringing into the world of the movie all kinds of other worlds: the worlds of other roles played by the star; the world of the star's real life as an actor; the world of the theater in which the audience is sitting (because to be a star is to be on a stage in front of a large, admiring audience); and the world of thousands of other theaters across the country in which people are also watching this star.[15] The supposedly sealed diegetic worlds of movies are cracked open by the presence of stars: scenes are set up, lit, photographed, and plotted to highlight the star quality of actors.

Central to the role of stars is their ability to draw crowds to movies, and we can see that filmmakers used this ability to define within movies themselves the proper kind of crowd. Consider, for example, the beginning of *Casablanca*: before we meet Rick, nightclub owner in the movie, we watch several people talk about him and say they want to meet him, and we hear his employee say that he never drinks with customers. We identify the character Rick as a star in the diegetic world of the movie; then we see him, and it is Humphrey Bogart, a star playing the role of a star. The first action Bogart does after we recognize him is to make two decisions about who gets into the club: he lets in a small-time crook, Ugarte, and keeps out a high-ranking Nazi. The movie thus suggests that being in the crowd around this star involves moral distinctions of a sort that we like—we will be allowed the thrill of small selfish crime and yet hold to high moral standards. We soon learn as well that Ugarte has killed two German couriers, in effect lining up with Rick against the Germans. Since Rick's club is devoted to entertainment, the opening scene of the movie projects the audience in the movie theater as part of a certain kind of crowd within the movie—fun-loving and free of Nazi influence—and similarly as part of a certain kind of crowd outside the movie, the crowd that makes Bogart a star by watching many of his movies. This small analysis brings out what the Hays Code says quite directly, that movie watching is not experienced entirely as a moment of isolation in the darkness; rather, a crucial part of movie watching is experiencing the sense of being part of a huge group all across the country watching the same images.

The Code was developed to solve the problem, as it sees it, that emerges from the way movies hail their audiences: once hailed, audiences supposedly become herd-like followers of almost any suggestion. The solution proposed is censorship, regulation of the morality represented in movies, particularly sexual and criminal morality. In effect, the Code proposes an ingenious way to avoid the consequences of the problem: if what people are given to follow is morally acceptable, then even if they do not have any moral resistance to it, it won't matter. The Code even suggests that by keeping movies moral, they will "improve the race."[16] In other words, this Code prescribes how to make use of the crowd response that makes everyone want to follow opinions expressed simultaneously all over the country, how to construct what Mill called a "second nature" in order to make morality a "custom."

Mill would not approve of this solution to the social tyranny produced by custom. He advocated restricting the power of prevailing opinion in order to leave people alone to make up their own minds. He pointedly rejected the notion of using the power of prevailing opinion to make people good. The Hays Code, contrary to Mill, does not propose leaving people alone at all, and does not even propose ways to help people resist the suggestions made by movies. It could propose, for example, transforming the distribution of films, say by releasing different movies in different areas of the country, so that no suggestion is made at once to people all over the country. Instead of trying to reduce the crowd response, the Hays Code focuses on how to use that response, which shows how individualism had changed since Mill's time. Mill's individualism is a political philosophy that calls for legal and political structures to block the social tyranny of the masses; the Hays Code instead uses the power of social influence to provide a common morality for everyone, a morality that favors the individual over the masses. Private life is no longer separated from public life but is instead constructed by it.

This transformation of individualism from a rejection of the crowd to a dependence on it is itself represented in Hollywood movies by two contradictory images of the crowd. The first, and most vivid, image is of a crowd that threatens individuality, the crowd that individuals must escape to become themselves. The second is of a crowd that supports the individual's escape. Let me give one surprising example of a Hollywood movie straining to reverse itself and recover a "good crowd" after it has condemned repeatedly and thoroughly the mindlessness of anonymous people gathered together. I turn to a movie presenting one of the most strident defenses of individualism of any Hollywood film—and an equally overt rejection of collectivism: *The Fountainhead*, from the book by Ayn Rand, who fled the USSR and wrote her novels to oppose collectivism in all forms. This movie seems to contrast the free individual, Howard Roark, avant-garde architect, with a collection of apparent cowards, who do not believe that individuals can stand against the crowd and so spend their time supporting traditional views that they don't really believe. These cowards are represented as tied to a newspaper that everyone agrees easily manipulates public opinion. The movie thus sets up a contrast between "genius," which constructs new things, and collective thought, which enforces old norms. Throughout the movie, both Roark and the toadies of the newspapers denigrate the average man as someone who lets himself be controlled. Roark seems to be a man who ignores collective opinion and goes his own way, with just enough independent backers to let him do his own work. When his designs are altered without his approval, he tries to get the buildings that result torn down and finally dynamites them. He is put on trial so that finally his freedom hinges on the decision of a jury of anonymous persons, who side with him after he makes an impassioned speech defending "individualism." My point is that Roark's (and Ayn Rand's) defense of individualism requires this anonymous support, this collective approval, in order to be the basis of a political system that supposedly opposes the kind of thinking that average, anonymous people do. We might expect the movie to reveal that the jurors are independent thinkers, but there is nothing in the movie that gives any clue to their minds at all. They appear only in collective shots, not even in close-ups of each thinking out his or her own ideas. There is no explanation for why this body of anonymous people thinks differently from the anonymous people so easily manipulated by the newspapers. We might presume that the reason this anonymous collective body can support individualism is that it is formed inside a legal system designed to protect an individual's rights. These people are safe from the insidious influence of the newspaper while they are sequestered on the jury, and perhaps that is why they are capable of independent judgment. Or we might conclude that the jury never thinks as independent individuals, that they simply come under the powerful influence of Roark's charisma and are swayed to the "right" conclusion. That would fit the Hays Code's view that the key to moral presentation of an issue to a crowd is that the person presenting it is moral: Roark's persuasion of the jury is simply the right kind of manipulation. The movie certainly takes that view towards its audience: it never risks exposing us to the newspaper. The audience only sees those who write the newspaper stating directly that they do not believe what they have written. Roark is the only person who believes in his own words and acts, and so the movie carefully keeps us in the jury box, insulated from the influence of widespread ideas. The movie carefully flatters its audience that we are in the "right" crowd, separated from the mindless group manipulated by mass media.

Though Roark claims to defend individualism, his appeal to the jury is not for them to think as separate individuals, as we might expect. Instead, he talks about the system of collectivism and its contrast to individualism: he asks them to vote for a social system, for individualism, and thus to join together with one coherent vision of what individualism is. The courtroom scene suggests what John Dewey says explicitly: that in the twentieth century, the complex architecture of the individualist social order cannot survive if everyone thinks only of their own private interests. Paradoxically "the individual" gets lost if there is nothing but a collection of completely isolated individuals:

> The tragedy of the "lost individual" is due to the fact that while individuals are now caught up into a vast complex of associations, there is no harmonious and coherent reflection of the import of these connections into the imaginative and emotional outlook on life. . . . The habit of opposing the corporate and collective to the individual tends to the persistent continuation of the confusion and uncertainty.[17]

Dewey goes on to say that the enslavement of individuals to a uniform social code, the evil individualism always opposes, derives in the twentieth century from the separation of individuals from a communal vision:

> Why should regimentation, the erection of an average struck from the opinions of large masses into regulative norms . . . be so characteristic of present American life? I see but one fundamental explanation. The individual cannot remain intellectually in a vacuum. If his ideas and beliefs are not the spontaneous function of a communal life in which he shares, a seeming consensus will be secured as a substitute by artificial and mechanical means.[18]

To produce a social order in which the ideas of individuals are "spontaneous functions" of a "communal life" while avoiding regimentation is a tricky proposition. But that is precisely the fine line Hollywood movies seek to walk. While the central plots show individuals resisting regimentation, the moviegoing experience aims at providing a sense of communal sharing, and somehow what is supposed to be shared is the belief in individuals resisting regimentation, so that the commonality of the support for individualism seems spontaneous, emerging from each and every member of the community separately. Twentieth-century individualism does not seek merely the freeing of individuals from coercive collective opinion; it seeks to create a communal life, a collective experience, which in some way produces and supports individuals in all their variety.

The individualism of Hollywood movies is usually considered to operate via a process of identification with the few stars at the center of the plot. But it is not simply a one-to-one identification that is going on. Like the jury in *The Fountainhead*, movie audiences are trained to collectively support the individuals with whom they identify. Identification is mediated by a process of first joining together with others in a collective,

21

nonpersonal identity and then slipping from that into one or a few persons with whom we "identify." I identify with someone who is not "me" by first merging with a body of persons who include "me" and this new person. Althusser made this point in his early work, *For Marx*:

> Before (psychologically) identifying itself with the hero, the spectatorial consciousness recognizes itself in the ideological content of the play, and in the forms characteristic of this content. Before becoming the occasion for an identification (an identification with self in the species of another), the performance is, fundamentally, the occasion for a cultural and ideological recognition. This self-recognition presupposes as its principle an essential identity (which makes the processes of psychological identification themselves possible, in so far as they are psychological): the identity uniting the spectators and actors assembled in the same place on the same evening. Yes, we are first united by an institution—the performance, but more deeply, by the same myths, the same themes, that govern us without our consent, by the same spontaneously lived ideology.[19]

The basis of identification is the sense of an undifferentiated identity bringing together everyone involved in the performance. We might say that everything that precedes the actual story—the titles and credits backed by symbolic visuals and music—is designed to serve this function. As people file into movie theaters, they usually come as separate "private" groups—members of a family or a few friends. The first task which moviemakers set themselves is to dissolve these interpersonal relations and set up instead what sociologist I. C. Jarvie calls an "unstructured group"—an audience.[20] The list of names indicates to the audience that the movie itself was produced by a crowd of people each of whom had a distinct function, but in fulfilling that function their distinctive personalities and private lives largely have faded away: they become a small version of the overall American social structure, producing what Althusser calls the "ideological recognition" that precedes identification. The audience members too drop their own personal distinguishing names as they watch the names of the creators of the movie all blur together. The music creates a common rhythm and emotion spreading over everyone: the audience becomes a group feeling "moved" together. After the movie has created this unstructured group reaction, the entire group can together get involved in supporting individuals in the pursuit of their own private goals: we pass from our private lives into an anonymous collective experience and then into other private lives.

A great deal of recent film theory has ignored this first step of ideological recognition preceding one-to-one identification; indeed, Althusser's later work has engendered a whole school of film analysis which seeks to show the reverse, that ideology is a result of one-to-one psychological identification. Critics draw on Althusser's concept of interpellation to transform analysis of ideology into analysis of interpersonal relationships, a move he himself supports by using Lacanian psychoanalysis to unpack the operation of ideology. But such a move turns the attention of critics toward characters and spectators as individual psychologies whose relationships are basically variations on sexualized family structures. The result is a strange vision of social issues, as if they were entirely a function of attitudes held by separate individuals locked together in peculiar familial relationships. The valuable critical method of looking for the social inside the personal seems to have resulted in the conclusion that there is nothing else but the personal.

A contradiction permeates such criticism: the imaginary world of the movie is entirely structured by personal, familial, characterological structures, while the world which is said to have constructed the film is entirely institutional and impersonal. Hollywood movies are then illusionary in a way that puts them almost entirely outside any debate about politics: all they are doing is covering up social issues, and the only reasonable political response must be to disrupt the vision they present: such is the conclusion drawn by critics such as Laura Mulvey and Colin MacCabe. MacCabe, drawing on Marxist theory, says that the world is structured by contradiction, but Hollywood movies "cannot deal with the real as contradictory."[21] So the only way to bring any touch of the "real" political scene into movies is to create avant-garde disruptive movies such as Godard's. Mulvey similarly argues that progressive politics requires "the decline of the traditional film form."[22]

In effect, such criticism finds the efforts to make movies supportive of their society's dominant ideology completely successful. But, as this book argues, Hollywood filmmakers found the structure of the movie experience so uncongenial to American ideology that they consciously placed within movies elements that undermined the political effects of that structure. And, as we shall see, supporters of alternative ideologies developed alternative structures, downplaying the elements that promoted individuality and highlighting the elements that produced a crowd response.

23

In Hollywood and "collectivist" movies alike, filmmakers struggled to control the contradictory political consequences of elements of their movies. Labeling the ideology of a film is not, then, as easy as film theorists would have it. And producing counter-Hollywood movies may not require acts as revolutionary as film theory would have it; reworking some contradictions within Hollywood films could lead to movies with quite different political effects. In Chapter 5, I examine an interesting case of a filmmaker who tries to alter the political effects of his movies by remaking them: Fritz Lang reached the bitter conclusion that external events had caused his early works to support the rise of Nazism, and so he decided at the end of his life to remake some of those movies to undo their "unintended" politics.

Recently, Colin MacCabe has called for a move away from psychoanalysis towards an analysis that relates movies to social movements. He writes in *High Theory/Low Culture* that the excitement of the oedipal analysis of ideology seems to be dying out, largely because everyone knows what it will reveal: "what I now want to consider is how one might pursue a radical interest in popular culture without limiting in advance the politics that will ensue from that interest."[23] In developing this call for a new kind of criticism, he distinguishes his approach from traditional Marxist approaches, which dismiss popular works as nothing but ideological illusion, and from what he calls the "optimistic" criticism of popular culture, which finds progressive political views in every popular work. These two opposed critical stances toward popular culture are equally useless, MacCabe argues, because they both conclude that the politics in popular works is already visible, already expressed, either in Marxist treatises or in the popular works themselves. In contrast, MacCabe calls for a study of popular culture based on the idea that the politics one seeks is not yet known to the critic nor apparent in popular texts. Rather peculiarly, this puts the critic in almost the same position as the filmmakers I am studying: seeking to understand how something within a work that is not visible to individual consciousness might energize millions of people to move together toward political goals. By analyzing the ways that filmmakers have tried to understand, represent, and control mass political reactions to their works, this book may contribute to critical projects such as MacCabe's and help critics not simply repeat what filmmakers have done. Critics need to consider how to build upon—or avoid—the historical conceptions of "crowd psychology," which are encoded into movies and have shaped the way we all understand social movements.

★   ★   ★

To begin to demonstrate the usefulness for film criticism of paying attention to the historical belief in collective spectatorship, I want to start by providing an alternative reading of a film that has been given one of the most detailed and brilliant explications of psychoanalytic/spectator theory: *Young Mr. Lincoln*. The editors of *Cahiers du Cinema* in 1970 produced a powerful Lacanian reading of that movie and found ways to connect its psychoanalytic structures to political issues contemporary with the movie.[24] Their analysis starts with a consideration of political issues facing the United States in the 1930s, turns to Hollywood's economic involvement with the Republican party, and then goes on to consider the movie as producing a vision of Lincoln, a Republican, as a transcendent moral figure, his eyes entirely on The Law even as he travels through a series of familial and sexual scenes. They emphasize that Lincoln is presented repeatedly with choices he does not make: he remains a transcendent spectator who stands beyond the choices other humans have to make, and indeed beyond politics and sexuality. Producing the movie thus supports the Republican cause against the New Deal, implying that the nation needs transcendent law, not governmental systems. Lincoln goes beyond being simply the greatest man: while most of the movie establishes that he is, as the authors of the article put it, capable of "castrating" every other man in the movie, such an act of standing above other men simply makes him, according to Lacanian theory, the most anxious about his covering up his own "lack." What makes Lincoln transcendent is that instead of being the biggest male around, he "is the phallus" and so is completely identified with The Law, transcendent of human dimensions entirely.[25]

Rather than arguing with this analysis, I want to draw attention to something else produced in this movie along with the sense of Lincoln as the transcendental spectator—and that is a crowd. We don't have to look very far to see a "crowd-in-the-text" giving mass responses to various scenes, because the movie is full of crowd scenes. The movie provides us with careful directions to distinguish between good crowds and bad ones, just as movies indicate which are good spectators and bad ones. Spectator theory has settled on gender as the crucial difference between good and bad spectators in Hollywood movies, but gender does not distinguish between crowds. Rather, as the Code suggests, the distinction is between those who are swept up in a frenzy without any individuals controlling themselves, and those who have settled into being spectators of a performance of individual actions. In *Young Mr. Lincoln*, the bad crowd is a lynch mob out to hang alleged murderers who knifed a man, and the good crowd is the same group of people seated during a trial as the real murderer is identified. In both cases, the crowd is seeking justice, a moral end, but in the first case they go out of control. Lincoln stops them, and one line he says that seems rather humorous might provide the best explanation of the difference between the two crowds: he says that he is happy to hang murderers, but he wants it done with some "legal pomp." The spirit of the crowd—the desire for moral revenge and the desire to see a hanging—has to be channeled into a certain kind of performance: the crowd has to become an audience responding to a show produced on a socially structured stage—the courtroom—rather than be the protagonist in a drama enacted on the unstructured streets of the city.

This does not mean the crowd has to learn to be silent and sit in the dark as spectators while the trial goes on. On the contrary, the trial is entirely presented in terms of the raucous and rowdy responses Lincoln's tricks and jokes elicit from the crowd. Lincoln plays the crowd as an entertainer, and in the climactic scene of the trial, he orchestrates a repetition of the spirit of the lynching. He does this when he seems to have lost the case, and as a last-ditch effort, recalls a witness, J. Palmer Cass, to the stand to repeat his testimony that he saw the murder performed in the moonlight. Lincoln seems to give up, tells Cass to step down, waits until Cass has opened the gate that separates the arena of lawyers, witnesses, and judge from the audience, and then turns on Cass and asks him why he committed the murder. Cass demurs, and Lincoln takes out an almanac to show that there was no moonlight the night of the murder, implying that Cass is lying, then asks again why Cass committed the murder. As Cass mumbles a response, the audience rises out of its seats and surrounds him, repeating the spirit of the lynching. Indeed, the man who was identified by Lincoln during the street scene as the bigmouth of the lynch mob, a fellow with the nickname "Big Buck," takes a central role in this semilegal proceeding by grabbing Cass from behind as Lincoln presses for a confession. Surrounded by an aroused crowd, literally in its clutches, the man confesses, and Lincoln then says, "your witness," indicating that this moment which seemed beyond the proper structure of court testimony was just an extended part of that structure. In other words, Lincoln, at the climax of his performance as entertainer/lawyer, orchestrates a crowd response akin to a lynching, redirecting the fervor that wanted revenge and hanging in the streets so that it presses a confession out of Cass. The mob is turned into an audience controlled by a masterful "entertainer," who even uses the tendency of crowds to get angry and rise up to get the performance necessary from the villain.

The movie defines the moment of Lincoln's almost magical victory as the moment which elevates him to the position of a star and so sets him on the way to being president. As he walks down the hall after the trial, he is told, "They are waiting for you," and steps into a doorway through which a bright light shines on him from outside, as we hear people cheering for him, though we don't see the crowd. What is enacted on the screen is the structure of the movie theater itself: a bright light shining over our shoulders as we watch a star appear in that light. This return to the crowd in the street joins us to the mob, but that mob has now become as invisible as we are, projected out just beyond the screen as the implied "crowd-in-the-text" which watches Lincoln's performance as an ideal movie audience.

Actually, the movie also shows that the crowd was performing as a peaceful audience before it became a lynch mob: the lynching came at the end of a day of festival celebration. The movie thus traces not only the transformation of lynch mob into audience by Lincoln's intervention, but the earlier transformation of audience into lynch mob. The cause of such a transformation is just what the Hays Code suggests: the incursion of improper sexuality and criminality into the scene of exciting entertainment. We could even describe this transformation as the improper incursion of private life into public spaces, the bad publicizing of private life. The movie shows this incursion by intercutting crowd scenes and small interpersonal scenes: the crowd watches Lincoln judge a pie contest; two hard cases, Scrub White and J. Palmer Cass, tickle a married woman; the crowd watches Lincoln split a log and start a tug-of-war; the woman's husband and his brother get angry at the hard cases; Lincoln cheats and wins the tug-of-war. As we watch, we experience a mixture of public entertainment and private scenes of improper sexual advances.

The alternation of crowd scenes and small interpersonal scenes becomes much more intense as night falls: one brother talks to his girl about getting married as he cuts into a log with the knife that will be the murder weapon, then the two brothers take a drink in front of the family campfire; crowds surround a bonfire in the dark; there is a fight between the two brothers and Scrub White, climaxing in Scrub dead and a knife from one of the brothers identified as the murder weapon; Cass cries out "Murder!" and the crowd around the bonfire, now holding torches, gathers at the murder scene, reacts, and heads off to arrange a lynching. The bonfire/fight/lynch mob scenes move so quickly that it is less than five minutes from bonfire to attempted lynching—and since torches appear throughout the mob after the cry of murder, it almost appears as if the bonfire has passed through the murder to become a crowd set aflame.

The buildup to the lynching scene thus traces the gradual mixing together of emotions derived from private scenes and emotions derived from crowd scenes. The emotions that fire the crowd begin as the emotions which fire the brothers: anger at immorality interrupting a day of exciting entertainment. Private motives are magnified into public action. The movie also highlights the central fear of the Hays Code, the danger of mixed audiences. Cass and Scrub are presented as a different kind of person mixed in with the wholesome townsfolk: they attend the festival but they refuse to join the crowd projected as responding to the festival. Instead of watching Lincoln, they watch a married woman. And the result of their being mixed in with the crowd at the festival is that entire crowd ends up transformed, breaking off from following the pleasant imagery provided by Lincoln and following instead a series of false suggestions orchestrated by Cass, the very person who refuses to accept the role as part of the crowd projected for him by the festival. The danger of sexuality and crime in this movie is not that deviant impulses lie deep inside everyone to be revealed when they are alone in the dark (as psychoanalytic theory would suggest); rather the danger is that sexuality and crime produce dangerous results when they are presented to people who are gathered in large groups aroused by watching a powerful light projected to produce spectacular entertainment—the bonfire, which becomes an image of movie projection (fig. 1).

The movie is then partly about the need to counter the power of movies themselves, of false images projected into a crowd by lights and words. The movie even seems to undermine the believability of its own physical scenes: when Lincoln uses a farmer's almanac to show there was no moon at the time of the fight, he raises serious doubts about what we ourselves saw on the screen, since we undoubtedly saw the fight lit up, much brighter than the ground around the bonfire. What the almanac shows, then, is that what we saw on the screen was not "reality" but a movie version of reality; the lights by which we saw the fight must have been movie lights, not anything natural at all. The movie itself is exposed as a liar just as Cass is. The sequence of scenes enacts what the Hays Code asks of Hollywood, letting us experience the power of movies to make us accept false suggestions and then reassuring us that Hollywood will use that power only to support morality.

The movie presents a message about the suggestibility of crowds, and this message aligns itself with the political concerns about crowds that

Fig.1. A bonfire as an image of movie projection.

permeated the 1930s. While the movie's invocation of lynch mobs certainly intersects with distinctively American politics in the South, most of the debate about crowds in the '30s was about the pressure toward collectivism worldwide as the Depression wore on. The main Republican answer to Roosevelt's radical policies was the claim that the New Deal was socializing America, giving in to collectivism, and destroying capitalist individualism. Against such a political backdrop, *Young Mr. Lincoln* gains most of its political power from its portrayal of the dangers of out-of-control crowds pursuing mistaken solutions to local problems. Lincoln is, as the editors of *Cahiers du Cinema* argue, used to bolster the image of Republicans, but he does so by resisting the appeal of crowd politics, of collectivism. Lincoln's admonishment to the lynch mob applies to the political crowds outside the movie theater reacting to the Depression: "We seem to lose our heads in times like this. We do things together that we'd be mighty ashamed to do by ourselves." The emotionally charged collective body threatens to destroy the individualist basis of morality.

We can also see the anticollectivist, anti–New Deal message of the movie in what the lynch mob is specifically trying to do: it would kill the two brothers who are small farmers. The editors of *Cahiers du Cinema* note that Republicans attacked the New Deal's biggest project, the Tennessee Valley Authority, as a threat to the American farmer, and conclude that Lincoln's use of a farmer's almanac to defend farmers aligns him with such Republican rhetoric. This interpretation can be carried further if we note that what Republicans said about the TVA is that it was a step toward socialism, towards collectivized farming a la Stalin. Lincoln is closest to Republican rhetoric, then, when he defends farmers against the aroused mob.

Lincoln does not, however, seem to be defending farmers against the mob so much as he is defending the family against the collective emotion of a large social body. The trial turns particularly on trying to distinguish between two brothers who are on trial, and one of the key witnesses is the mother, who, we are led to believe, actually does know which brother committed the crime, but will not speak. In other words, the case seems to be aiming at watching a family break apart, due to murderous impulses related to sexuality within that family. For most of the movie, we are led by cues such as the mother's behavior to believe that one of the brothers did commit the murder: in other words, the movie itself creates the effect on us of the "mass suggestion" that seems to have infected everyone except Lincoln, to believe that the death of Scrub was a result of the fight. The mother saw almost exactly what we saw. Her refusal to testify is in effect a denial of the "truth" which the movie itself seems to have shown us—a refusal to participate in the movie experience itself. But much as the movie gives the audience the desire to stand with the mother, we are also set up to see her as refusing to accept reality. We cannot simply assert the value of the private family against the public call for justice. And by the end, when the true killer is revealed, the movie has shown us that the private sphere itself has been distorted by the public events: the mother did not see what she thought she saw. Her testimony would actually have been mistaken (as our view of the fight was mistaken). She was in fact caught up in the mass "suggestion" as much as the rest of the town.

So what the movie finally does to restore our belief in the family is not to separate the private and the public, but rather to coordinate the two, to bring the public and the private back into alignment, through a public performance which bequeaths the right kind of private world to the family. And the figure who can orchestrate the public world so that it produces once again the right kind of private sphere is Lincoln, a figure who seems capable of crossing all the bounds between spheres, including even the bound between the movie and "real history," as the last few shots indicate. Lincoln goes up a hill, watches lightning flare up, and then walks off into the flashing light as the *Battle Hymn of the Republic* rises in volume (fig. 2). Then the scene dissolves to the Lincoln Monument, with Lincoln's eyes like dark holes in the screen (fig. 3). This ending reminds us that Lincoln is going off to his greatest role and to his death, and in doing so he is transcending physical reality as it has been represented in the movie thus far. The ending is not simply the closure of the story but a revision of the very form of this movie, stepping beyond its "realism." Lincoln goes off to a supernatural realm, a realm where one can see beyond what is visible into the dark realm of truth and monumentally stable morality. This transition takes two steps: first he enters a mysterious natural realm that seems to lead outside of the whole world of the people we have been watching, and then he is transmuted from this extrasocial "nature" into the utterly impersonal realm of a monumental national figure, becoming an image that we already know and already trust more than we trust our own eyes. The ending in effect symbolizes what the Hays Code promises: that before we even enter a Hollywood movie, we can trust that American values will stand behind the story, and thus we can allow the movie to temporarily mislead us and reduce our ability to stand by our own morality (i.e., reduce our "moral resistance"). Hollywood studios do not ask the audience to trust what is shown on the screen; instead they ask viewers to trust the American industry, which agrees to resist the power of the reality portrayed on the screen and provide a moral base outside that reality. At the end of this movie, Lincoln passes into this other reality, becoming in effect an image of the solidity of the entire American film industry, which strives to present itself as monumentally trustworthy, a collective institution that ensures that each individual filmmaker will keep his or her eyes on the darkness where morality is entombed outside all the false lighting of every movie.

Figs 2–3. Lincoln disappearing into the light . . .

and reappearing as a dark monument.

2

CONSTRUCTING PUBLIC INSTITUTIONS AND PRIVATE SEXUALITY: THE BIRTH OF A NATION AND INTOLERANCE

*T*he *Birth of a Nation* was the first blockbuster hit, setting sales records in 1915 that were not surpassed for years. The movie has mostly been interpreted in terms of racial politics because of its intimate relationship with the Ku Klux Klan, which used it to recruit members. But the movie intersects as well with some very different political movements that filled the news in 1915: socialist, labor, and communist parties. If we consider the movie in terms of the United States' coming to understand itself in opposition to collectivism, we can make sense of the unusual structure of the film. Collectivism called for the government to think in terms of the social totality rather than individual interests. Individualists responded that the result of such governmental actions was invasion and interference with private life, disrupting the operation of individual desires. During the nineteenth century, individualists argued simply for the government and all social forces to stay out of private lives. But in the twentieth century, the belief that the nation was held together by crowd emotions led to the conclusion that if all social forces were removed, the nation would simply fall apart. Indeed, as we saw in Chapter 1, John Dewey argued that increasing the isolation of individuals from each other would result in a social order of mechanical regimentation, and Herbert Blumer argued that stripped of social categories, individuals would become a "mob." Crowd psychology implied that a "communal emotion" was needed to allow individuals to be individuals, contradictory as that might seem. Hollywood movies developed a way to make sense of this para-doxical belief, by showing that certain kinds of social structures led to certain kinds of private lives.

The Birth of a Nation represents the history of civil rights in terms of the effect on private lives of shifts in vast institutional structures. The Civil War interferes with what the movie goes to great lengths to show are "good" love affairs (between whites of two wealthy families); Recon-struction produces "bad" love affairs (cross-racial, cross-class sexual as-saults); and the construction of the KKK restores the good ones. So the movie develops a three-part analysis of the connection between certain kinds of national institutions and private love affairs. Indeed, as the title suggests, the United States did not even become a nation until the KKK was developed to counter the bad effects of certain social policies which the movie describes as producing "disunion." This movie suggests that "union" is only possible in a nation when love affairs are kept strictly within racial boundaries. Mixing races disrupts all families, even those which were entirely within one "race" before the mixing.

The threat to the United States of racial integration is represented in the movie, then, as the collective interference with the ideal forms of individual relationships, with free choice in love (which, the movie im-plies, always follows racial lines). The climactic evil of this movie is the destruction of private life, represented visually as collective structures—crowds—replacing private houses. War is represented first in terms of people leaving their houses to join together in large gatherings—balls, bonfires, and parades, celebrating armies marching off; then these excited gatherings are replaced by battle scenes that reduce everyone to dots. Reconstruction is presented as mixed-race crowds breaking into private houses. Battles return at the end, but these are fought by the KKK to restore private life, protecting a cabin in the woods from invasion by an army and rescuing a woman from forced marriage.

After the historical sequences, the movie leaves realism behind to alle-gorically summarize the development of the United States as both the final possibility of a happily married couple and the end of dictatorial and false authority—as if the period traced in the film, the Reconstruction, were the final phase of the separation of the United States from British monarchy. We see a happily married couple talking together by the sea, and the man, Ben Cameron, inventor of the KKK, says,

Dare we dream of a golden day when the bestial War shall rule no more.

But instead—the gentle Prince in the Hall of Brotherly Love in the City of Peace.

This title card is followed by two parallel scenes, one of a giant man on horseback (or perhaps a centaur) with a sword swinging at much smaller people fighting below, cutting a swath of dead bodies; then a scene of a giant Jesus with arms raised blessing people, all dressed in white robes and dancing. The title card itself is arranged in two sentences/paragraphs set above each other, as many titles in this movie are—and the two lines define a contrast as the two scenes do, creating verbally and visually a basic structure of argument, of rhetoric, advocating something by showing it is better than something else. This final allegorical argument seems to oppose two kinds of superhuman rulers, warlike and gentle, which would seem to indicate that the goal of the movie is an ideal leader, not an individualist social order. The movie certainly does set one leader against another: Ben, the creator of the KKK, saves the country from Austin Stoneman, whose Reconstruction policies threaten the entire nation. But Ben is not simply a substitute for the president and Congress: he never assumes a political role in the visible government; instead he leads the KKK in secret and leaves the government in other hands. The movie's ending suggests that great visible leadership is not the ultimate goal. The allegorical scenes do not end with Jesus standing above everyone. Rather, the image of Jesus fades out, leaving the people happily dancing without any leader at all. Then the scene of people dancing dissolves into an image of buildings on a hill—the City of Peace, appearing as a collective structure. Finally, there is a cut to the married couple staring off into space while the image of the City appears next to them floating in the sky, appearing to be what the two of them are imagining. This final sequence suggests that the movie does not aim at replacing the evil leadership of the war god with the good leadership of Jesus; rather it wants to go beyond giant leader-figures entirely, to a system of government that operates by being installed inside the minds of married couples, inside the private home. Government operates then not as an external structure looming over the nation, but as an internal structure of every individual household. The end of giant leadership (i.e., monarchy) is one with the arrival of the private family and that is only possible with racial unity, so that "love" does not assume a perverse form. The movie's logic is based on a precise assumption, that love is a "natural" emotion, which, if left alone by the social surroundings, will flow to persons of the same race. It is false "crowd emotions," which cause people to "lose their heads" and begin mixing races together.

35

After the final image of the couple, there is a final title card which summarizes the movie's theory of merging the private and the public:

"<u>Liberty and union</u>,
one and inseparable,
<u>now</u> and <u>forever</u>!"

These final words mirror the structure of the final shot of the couple imagining the City: both the shot and the final words are divided between collective and individual realms. The words are in three pairs, each pair bringing together an "individual" and a "collective" quality. In the first pair, "liberty" implies the freedom of each separate person (or each separate state) to determine its own desires, and "union" implies the collecting together of like persons according to those free desires, in marriage and in the union of white states in the nation. "One and inseparable" again implies a wholeness of several parts; finally, "now and forever" merges the singularity of a moment with the eternality of a principle: what is being advocated is not merely this particular couple or the particular states at one moment, but something that transcends all individuals. Marriage represents the merger of liberty and union by being presented as the free choices of the two partners to join together; its opposite is forced marriage or rape. And paralleling this private world are two public issues: first, the union of the states; and second, the mixing of black and white races. Are these two unions freely chosen or are they shotgun marriages? These two public issues are used in the movie to represent the two opposed ways of bringing people together: the plot shows that the north and south can join freely, preserving liberty, because they are really "brothers" though they may at times battle; black and white, however, can only be yoked together in shotgun marriages—or rapes—because, according to this movie, their relations can never be "brotherly love." As we shall see, the movie implies that there can never be love, or freely chosen sexual desire, between black and white, and that puts a "natural" limit on the extension of the free state. The decision to exclude blacks from public life is then simply a corollary of individualism, a social order which exists above all to allow "free" choice of associations in private life and to eliminate forced associations.

The overall plot of the movie is constructed to show that it was a mistaken national policy of forcing mergers of people who are not in some broad sense "brothers" that caused the Civil War. The opening title states bluntly that bringing the "African" to America sowed the seeds of "disunion." The images used to represent "disunion" are not images of people being forced apart, but rather of people being brought together in ways that appear pleasant but are (the movie will eventually reveal) bad. "Disunion" is a "diseased union" resulting from the mistake of uniting persons who do not in some natural way belong together. The opening scenes rather bizarrely suggest that slavers and abolitionists all made the same mistake because they all aimed at keeping blacks and whites living together. The slavers and abolitionists are introduced in parallel scenes of whites standing with their arms above blacks in gestures that appear to be blessing or embrace. The images suggest peaceful, nearly familial relations, but the titles identify these images as "disunions," mergers that are the germs of later disasters. As the plot progresses, we learn that it is precisely the seeming kindness of the contacts in the opening shots that defines the problem. This mistaken uniting of different races eventuates in the destruction of the individualist social order, the wrecking of private life, by leading to the eruption of bad sexual desire. Sexuality first is introduced in a shot which is labeled "The great leader's weakness that is to blight a nation": the shot shows Austin Stoneman being more than friendly to Lydia Brown, a "mulatta." This shot could be interpreted as implying that the source of the national disaster is a personal problem, but the sequence leading up to this shot puts Stoneman's desire as the logical outcome of a series of relationships: he is positioned to Lydia as both the slavers and the abolitionists were positioned to the blacks in the earlier shots. His "weakness" is thus presented as an outgrowth of a long history of mistaken uniting of black and white, the effect and not the cause of "disunion."

The movie then traces the disastrous effects upon private, familial, and sexual relationships of the social policy promoted by Austin Stoneman, the policy of different races living together peaceably.[1] First the movie focuses on how that policy wrecks "brotherly love" by showing the Civil War erupting. The war is presented primarily in terms of its disruption of domestic life. As for military action, we see only three scenes of soldiers using their weapons: the first is the invasion of Piedmont by the irregulars, which is presented through cross-cutting scenes of wild soldiers in the streets and women cowering in their houses; eventually the soldiers invade the houses. The second scene is the extended battle that is presented as an effort by the South to get food to its starving soldiers. The third is a long-distance shot of soldiers rampaging, and that one is titled "the torch of war against the breast of Atlanta"; intercut with the long shots are shots of women and children hiding in bushes. Thus, the only fighting we see is presented entirely as northern interference with southern domestic life, with women, children, private houses, and food.

Griffith's structuring of the battle scenes helps us understand them entirely in terms of their interference with private lives. In the extended battle scene, the chaotic camera-shots that show gunfire and smoke over a huge area give us no clue what is happening in the battle, but intercut into these long shots are two crucial sequences that present personal consequences of the war. First is an image of the younger brothers from the Stoneman and Cameron families dying in each other's arms, a tender embrace in death ironically described by the title card, "Chums meet again." Then the elder brothers of these same families meet up with each other, as Ben leads a hopeless charge against Phil Stoneman's troops. Along the way, Ben risks his own life to give water to an enemy soldier, and after that, everyone cheers Ben so that when he enters the enemy lines, Phil stops the troops from killing him. The scenes define war as the disruption of the ties of family and friends, and hence inherently wrong. To recognize friendship, as Phil does, is to violate the ethics of war. These two sequences mirror the sequence of the final two allegorical scenes: first a scene of slaughter, then a scene of brotherly union. The older brothers of these two families succeed in overcoming the "disunifying" effects of war and of U.S. history since the introduction of Africans to the country, and so model what the movie wishes to advocate: that governmental actions should not disrupt private life.

After that extended battle, we see further effects of the war on domestic life: women selling their clothes "for the failing cause" and "the torch of war against the breast of Atlanta"—as if the violence were directed against women. War is summarized as "bitter, useless sacrifice" and "breeder of hate"—shown through the little sister's anger—and the sacrifices we see are all familial. The end of the war does not bring about the restoration of private life, because the images of war continue to interfere with love. The older Cameron daughter, Margaret, cannot respond to her suitor, Phil Stoneman, because, as the titles declare, the "bitter memories will not allow the poor bruised heart of the South to forget": as Phil approaches her, she looks away and an insert shows what is in her mind—a soldier dying (figs. 4 and 5).

The cure for Margaret's trauma, it turns out, is a second trauma, a second war scene, one that restores what the Civil war broke apart: the union of northern and southern whites. This second war scene takes place at the climax of the movie, when she finds herself trapped in a cabin with Phil and with some white ex-union soldiers, all under assault by black troops. As the blacks are about to burst the cabin door open, she suddenly falls into Phil's arms and finds herself feeling once again the

Figs. 4–5. Margaret unable to respond . . .

because of what her bruised heart is seeing.

joy of being with him. Her subplot traces quite bluntly the shaping of sexual desires by social policy: when the whites are divided and killing each other, love cannot flourish because the heart of each white person will be full of images of horror. When the whites unite in their war against blacks, then true love between a white couple is possible. So some kinds of wars break up families and love (those that divide a single race) and other kinds of wars restore families and love (those that separate different races).

A similar mininarrative is traced in the affections of Elsie Stoneman for Ben: she turns from him when she discovers his involvement in the KKK because she feels honor-bound to support her father's policies. Her reaction is not as involuntary as the Cameron daughter: she does not like rejecting Ben, but she does so for her father's principles. She loses her scruples and recovers her active love when Ben rescues her from being forced to marry the black leader Silas Lynch. Actually, she does not so much overcome her principled resistance to Ben as find that the source of that principle—her father—changes his mind: Austin Stoneman discovers in her capture and her rescue that he too welcomes the KKK. The Stonemans have to experience horror to discover the familial and sexual consequences of their principles.

There is a second effect of the Reconstruction period on private lives: it leads to the eruption of desires so strong they lead to rape or forced marriage. The movie is quite direct in stating that this kind of desire is a result of bad social policy. The first person introduced with such desires is Gus, who is described in a title as a "renegade, a product of the vicious doctrines spread by the carpetbaggers." He is a mulatto who peers at white women from behind trees and then pursues them forcibly. Calling Gus a "renegade" suggests that perhaps he is just an accidental by-product of the vicious policies, something that could be solved by adding in a kind of police force. However, the attempt to "police" Gus—represented by Ben's chasing after him as he pursues Ben's sister—fails, resulting in the death of the woman. The scene shows that Ben's efforts as a private person, a real brother, are too late; allegorically such efforts are too late because they come after the social policies that are creating the problems. What is needed is not simply policing, but a different social policy, represented in this movie as requiring a supplemental institution (the KKK) in addition to the formal government. The movie goes on to trace the emergence of this institution, but it introduces the need for it by showing a second person gaining what the movie codes as improper sexual desires from public policy, and this second person is not merely a misfit who could be controlled by policing; instead, it is the very leader at the center of the policy, Silas Lynch, who assaults Elsie Stoneman.

Silas assaults Elsie immediately after pardoning Austin Stoneman, a scene which parallels an earlier moment when Lincoln pardoned Ben Cameron at the urging of Ben's mother. Both scenes focus on the power given leaders to transcend the laws, a power that threatens to convert elected leaders into kings and so undermine the individualist system that puts laws above leaders. And it is precisely in terms of a wish to convert the elected system into a feudal one that Silas proposes marriage to Elsie immediately after granting the pardon: he offers to make her his "queen" in a "black empire." When this offer fails to incite her desire for him, he becomes enraged and assaults her, using his assistants to hold her for him.

Silas's assault fails because Ben saves her. This second attempt at rescuing a white woman from assault by a black man succeeds because this time Ben does not simply act as a private citizen: instead he sets up a counter-regime, the KKK, which a title card quoting Woodrow Wilson calls "a veritable empire of the South." Most intriguing is the way that this movie shows this "veritable empire" functioning: the crucial feature of its operation, it turns out, is precisely that it seeks to intervene at that crucial juncture between public and private, that moment that the movie ends on, the installation of a vision of a social order inside the heads of individuals. The KKK is not an alternative government: it does not provide different laws or deliver different services. Rather, it is a social institution that functions by creating effects inside individual psychologies while leaving the laws of the rest of society in place. It is a social institution for the construction and installation of fantasies. Ben discovers the methodology for the KKK's operation from watching children play: he sees the power of kids in white sheets to scare black kids. From that moment, he develops the idea of adults wearing white sheets to terrify blacks, and then he goes on to find rituals that serve to instill the power to terrify into the minds of the whites who will wear those sheets: he has them gather around burning crosses, and he dips into the blood of his dead sister to inspire them.

The movie shows, then, the building of an institution for psychological influence; such an institution is the central feature of the "birth of a nation." Thomas Dixon, author of the novel on which the movie was based, declared that the point of the movie was to "create a feeling of abhorrence in white people, especially white women, against colored men."[2] An institution that can create such powerful feelings can counter the actual flow of real political history, the changes in social structure due to bad doctrines that nonetheless remain legally in force. The KKK in this movie does not go to war the way the North did, and its success is not simply a military victory (though it does borrow the imagery of military victory): rather, it performs a series of symbolic acts. Indeed, one might say it constructs a movie, giving costumes to certain people so they can perform visual displays, turning ordinary people into "stars," using powerful visual and visceral imagery (fiery crosses and the blood of a dead woman) to produce reactions in hundreds of people sitting and watching, and, finally, enacting narratives that have symbolic power but do not actually change the legal structures (such as flinging lynched bodies on political doorsteps).

The movie thus implies that institutions such as movies are crucial in maintaining the American social order. The need for such institutions modifies the individualism of the central love stories. The movie remains fundamentally individualist in portraying the final goal of all social policy to be good private lives, good marriages. But it suggests that individuals must be supported by quasi-governmental institutions that provide images of a good collective structure of the nation. In such institutions, individuals give up their individual identities to create the image of the collective—they hood themselves to make a mass of identical white bodies. The movie suggests then that a rather distinctly nonindividualist kind of social institution is necessary to allow individualism to exist. The KKK in this movie is a social institution for the construction and installation of fantasies in order to allow capitalist individualism to exist, precisely an Ideological State Apparatus in Althusser's terms. The "birth of the nation" is then the birth of the proper images of the nation, as a collection of identical white bodies.

The final allegorical images of this movie are not, then, simply allegories. They are the most literal images of the movie, because they are presented as simply images, not representations of other "real" things: they represent the fundamental function of this movie, which is to provide images to be taken away by members of the audience. This movie is about the way that images are installed inside people by social institutions, and how those images affect private lives. What appears as allegorical and not real—the images of evil giants and of Jesus—are rather the real agents through which social orders operate, particularly in the individualist age, when there are no longer actual giant leaders who can simply command. Without giant leaders, we need giant images—and complex institutions which create those images. The movie is the story of how historical institutions create fantasies and the roles that those fantasies then play within history. The operation of fantasy on real events is to turn those events into allegories, so the movie is in some sense about how real history is created by the construction of allegories.

The important function of fantasy in the construction of history within this movie undermines the typical film theory idea that "realism" is the vehicle by which movies carry out their ideological projects. The role of fantasy also undermines this movie's own claim to a more mundane kind of "realism"—the claim to be based on history. The tension between what is realistically historical and what is fictional appears repeatedly in the construction of scenes and of title cards in this movie. The scenes most celebrated as realistic in this movie—the war scenes—are the ones most interrupted by extremely unrealistic fictional events. The scene of the two young brothers dying in each others' arms is obviously unrealistic; it stands out as an emotional symbol grafted on to historical war scenes, which by themselves seem to be almost meaningless. There is created in such moments a strong sense that Griffith is moving beyond the historical accuracy of the war scenes (and other scenes that the movie footnotes as derived from historical texts). A huge apparatus of research and filmic construction is being brought to bear to create meaningful fantasy out of history, and in particular to install into the audience's heads the images that will allow us to feel brotherly love and avoid war—by having the right kinds of public and private desires.

The principles the movie is advocating are clearly associated then with the fictional or fantasy quality of the movie, with its constructedness, its disruption of footnoted accuracy, its rhetorical parallels, while what it opposes—the mixture of races in the United States, the Civil War—has the quality of being simply historically true. Disunion, loveless relationships—these are the gist of history; brotherly union is the gist of fantasy. The acts of the KKK, like the acts of the moviemakers, are acts of constructing fantasies and implementing institutional procedures to make those fantasies appear in the minds of vast numbers of people in order to counteract legal and political structures that remain as historical facts but will function in quite different ways because of these fantasies.

I suggest that the need for nonrealistic images—for allegory—is part of the new forms of individualism (and collectivism) emerging in the twentieth century. Individualism and realism seemed to belong together in the nineteenth century, both based on the presumption that real objects exist as particulars, individuals, so that all collective structures are merely abstractions created by speaking of many individuals all at once. At the turn of the twentieth century, however, there developed a strong recognition that there must be transindividual elements which are not simply as collections of individuals. Such transindividual elements cannot be quite real, that is, they cannot be located in physical objects, which seem to exist only as separate individual bodies. Instead, the transindividual elements exist in the category of the collective imagination and in this movie appear when the individuals mask themselves into the collective body of the KKK. As cited in Chapter 1, John Dewey, staunch defender of individualism, noted the need for some collective imaginary, for a "coherent and harmonious reflection" of the "connections" among persons. Without an imaginary "reflection" of the social order, individuals become "lost"; with the collective imaginary, the "ideas and beliefs" of the individual become the "spontaneous function of a communal life in which he shares."[3] The contrast Dewey describes between a "spontaneous" community and a world of "lost" individuals is what *The Birth of a Nation* portrays in the contrast between the world of whites and the world of mixed races. The first half of the movie, the Civil War and Lincoln's death, sets up the breaking up of the "spontaneous" community of the United States, creating "lost individuals" such as all the young Camerons and Stonemans who cannot love each other. The KKK, as the agency creating the communal vision Dewey advocates, becomes, in this movie, the agent of the restoration of individualism.

Such a conclusion is not as strange as it may sound: the argument for individualism in Hollywood movies usually ends up showing two or more persons who are "like" each other coming together (usually in a happy kiss) and separating from some other persons who are "unlike" them (the villains). Hollywood's individualism is thus not an argument for letting everyone think in different ways. It is hard to even imagine a story which had as a happy ending everyone simply going their different ways; rather, successful individualism is usually represented as the freely coming together of persons who discover they already think alike. So in a strange way, images of significant difference end up being associated with anti-individualism (forced association), and images of a group of people finally all seeming alike end up being associated with individualism, with free choice. To create the sense that achieving that final unity is a battle for freedom worth fighting, the choice of those persons to join together can never be simply a result of some shared idiosyncrasies; there must be something deeply shared, something beyond their individuality, and that something tends to be represented as a bodily type; race in this movie, beauty in many other movies. Hence there is a residue in nearly all Hollywood movies of what this movie reveals so bluntly, an almost inherent ethnocentrism inside twentieth-century individualism.

Griffith implies moreover that a deeply shared ethnic quality is not by itself enough to secure the proper form of private lives: an institution is necessary to allow expression of the "natural" desires which should flow from such ethnic similarity. Until the KKK is constructed, desires that should unite individuals become seriously misguided, as we see in the estrangement of the two white couples, Elsie and Ben and Margaret and Phil. Without an institution shaping individual desires, individualism simply goes awry. *The Birth of a Nation* traces the history of a misguided "individualism"—one which is based on the belief that individuals can be freed from all social categories and thus cross all social boundaries.

Griffith's next movie, *Intolerance*, traces a much longer history of public institutions which have shaped desire, presenting the last several thousand years in terms of the separation of public and private forms of sexuality. Miriam Hansen describes this movie as an anxious warning against the dangers of unmarried women, whose sexuality is not contained in private space.[4] I would recast this description to say the movie is about the power of unmarried women, a power that can be extremely useful to the state—or extremely destructive. In the first, longest story, of Babylon, an unmarried woman, the Mountain Girl, starts off a bit disruptive in her unwillingness to marry, but what the movie traces is how her standing apart from the usual path leads to her becoming the one hope for saving the state. Her story demonstrates that an unmarried woman can fulfill a very useful social role, and may even embody an ideal to which everyone else should aspire. She provides a sharp contrast to the unmarried woman in modern times, represented by the Friendless One. Their two names identify the crucial difference between them: in modern times, a woman unmarried is cut off from everyone else—friendless—so her desires have nowhere to go but into social disruption. She becomes a killer and a disruption of marriage. In Babylon, by contrast, the unmarried woman may be disconnected from the people around her, but that does not leave her "friendless," rather she has instead a relation to the "mountain," to something huge and impersonal that can provide a socially useful role for her to play. As in *Bergfilm* in Germany, the relation of the woman to the mountain is a vision of a social sexuality, of the channeling of a woman's desires into an impersonal social end instead of into a single relationship to one man (as we will see in the next chapter's discussion of *The Blue Light* by Leni Riefenstahl). When the Mountain Girl is freed from marriage, from private sexuality, she discovers a public sexuality, a love for the state, for the king. What Babylon has that no other society in this movie has is this public sexuality into which individuals can invest their desires. Griffith spends considerable time showing celebrations in which Belshazzar, the Babylonian king, is surrounded by crowds of women in highly sexualized rituals. An unmarried woman can love the king without competing with the king's beloved for his body, because this society has public rituals of sexuality in relation to the king. Sexuality is not restricted to two-person private lives, but becomes a crowd phenomenon. As Lesley Brill notes, the "sexy, pleasure-celebrating crowds in Babylon embody not decadence but the springing up and increase of life."[5]

In Babylon, being separated from one's familial role does not leave one alienated and adrift, as it does in the modern world. The failure of the Mountain Girl to save the kingdom marks the end of this public sexuality, and the separation of the social order into private lives and public structures. People can no longer have a relationship to the vast "ground" upon which the state rests—to the mountain—but only to various "friends."

The two eras presented after Babylon and before modern times show the increasing separation of public and private, and the gradual reduction of any possibility of there being a "public" desire. In the first story after Babylon, set in the biblical era, the problem of a woman's sexuality outside of marriage arises as well, in the scene of the adulterous woman who would be stoned. When Jesus saves her, he is suggesting that through him, through a love for his supraindividual body, extramarital sexuality (of women in particular) can be purged of its destructive force. Jesus becomes, as he was in the final images of *The Birth of a Nation*, the substitute for the larger-than-human figures of kings and emperors. Jesus is still a larger-than-human figure, but not one who remains physically present as the leader of a nation; rather, his religion becomes a supplement to various governments, providing a king-like figure to be "loved" as kings themselves disappear.

In the tale of Jesus, Griffith begins to show the reduction of the glory and power of leaders. The public figures we see—the Pharisees—do not bring everyone together in public rituals. Instead, their acts simply interrupt various moments of private life. The first introduction of the Pharisees shows them causing persons who are engaged in private activities—working, eating—having to freeze in place awkwardly and painfully as a Pharisee prays in public. This is a world devoid of a unifying public ritual such as Babylon had. Even more important, it is a world devoid of public sexuality and pleasure. Most of what the Pharisees end up representing is antipleasure and antisexuality, and Jesus is presented as finding ways to preserve some of what has been lost. Jesus provides wine for a wedding after the Pharisees call wine-drinking bad; he saves the adulterous woman the Pharisees would kill; and he tells people to be like doves, an image that alludes back to Belshazzar, who gave his beloved princess a dove. Note, though, that unlike Belshazzar's rituals, Jesus's rituals of drinking, loving, and being like doves are not part of a public or group pleasure. Jesus is not a figure setting up public rituals to replace those of the Pharisees; rather he is transferring some of what was in Belshazzar's public rituals to the realm of private life, to supplement the dry public religion of the Pharisees. Jesus's death thus does not eliminate his role, as did the death of Belshazzar; rather, Jesus is still available as an image to love, and loving him becomes a way of living according to a set of codes which underlie modern society—and so the tales after Jesus are all set in Christian countries.

The next tale in historical sequence after Jesus is a tale about the breakdown of the unified image which he provided, the division of the religion created in his name. The tale represents this division as deriving from the loss of a ritual of public sexuality. In France in 1652, the division between Catholic and Huguenot in France could be healed by a public marriage between royal children from the two different groups. Such a marriage would provide a public ritual of sexuality that could bring together the unfulfilled desires of all in the nation, and keep those desires from turning into the "perverse" form of desire—violence. But blocking this marriage is an unmarried woman, the king's mother, who, having lost her husband, does not turn to what I have been calling the public forms of sexuality, to love for Jesus or love for the couple who could unite the nation; rather she turns to what this movie codes as a perverse form of private love—she loves her son who is homosexual and seeks to install him in place of the couple whose marriage would bring peace. Her acts divorce leadership from the ritual of public sexuality that the marriage would provide and so the two groups join in war instead of marriage.

The modern story shows the complete breakdown of the relationship of sexuality to public life which was the basis of Babylon. And once again this is coded as a problem of unmarried women, who cannot find any leaders or public images in which to invest their sexuality. The modern era starts by showing large numbers of such women, who have become reformers, "uplifters," because, the movie states quite baldly, they have no men. While this statement certainly shows Griffith's sexism, it also implies that the "uplifters" are in fact trying to do what used to be possible—to find satisfaction by investing their sexual desires in public acts.

But in the modern world this becomes a disaster, because modern male leader-figures have no "public sexuality" in which to invest; sexuality is entirely divorced from leadership and contained within private life. In such a world, putting personal desires into public events simply distorts everything, and the effects of the influence of unmarried women upon the industrial leader (a brother of one of the uplifters) are economic failures and then strikes. The movie implies that strikes and economic disasters do not derive from the structure of industry at all, but from the absence of a public institution into which unmarried women could invest their desires.

The actions of the uplifters in public spheres parallel the actions of the Friendless One in private spheres. The Friendless One is, like the uplifters, unable to find a man and so her sexuality turns to destructive acts. As the uplifters support bad industry policies, the Friendless One supports a gang of criminals; as the uplifters break up the marriage between the girl and the boy, the Friendless One nearly makes the breakup permanent by causing the boy to be accused of murder. And when the Friendless One confesses, she somehow undoes not only her crime but those of the uplifters, and points toward what could be a general solution to the problem of unattached desire: her confession derives from her discovery of Jesus as the object of her love instead of the gang leader or the boy, and it is this love for a disembodied image, for a religious icon, for a public figure, that restores order.

However, the movie does not go on to show a similar conversion of the uplifters, and so the movie gives no evidence that belief in Jesus would provide a broad solution to desires that cannot be satisfied in marriage. Jesus as the embodiment of a public ritual of love just doesn't seem as available in the modern world as Belshazzar was in the ancient world, with the result that, in the modern era, the unmarried woman discovers Jesus only as she goes to her death. Jesus does not give unmarried women a role in the state, as Belshazzar did in Babylon, but rather provides a way for them to withdraw. The Friendless One's discovery of the right sort of love allows her to undo the damage she has done, but not to save the state, as the Mountain Girl's love almost did. The movie suggests that something else is needed besides religion in the modern world, and we can see what that is in considering how much has to happen after the Friendless One confesses to save the boy: her confession needs to be conveyed to the governor and then the governor's word has to be conveyed to the boy's prison in order to stop the boy's execution. In other words, her confession needs to be supplemented by a "medium" for transmitting what she has to say, and that medium operates by connecting together individuals and public figures.

The movie does not simply show a series of messages being transmitted; rather, the conveyance of the confession to the governor and his pardon to the prison is shown in terms of a long chase sequence. At first it seems that what is being chased is the governor, but what we watch is not a person being searched for and found; the person, the body of the governor, appears only very briefly and seems merely another cog in the mechanics of the chase, a device for passing the message of the boy's innocence to the prison. What we actually watch in the chase are not persons at all, but rather two machines, an automobile and a train. The train, I suggest, is an image of public technology, moving crowds of people through society, in contrast to the automobile, which is very much a vehicle for carrying families around. In a sense then the chase represents the desire to connect together the technology for moving crowds to the technology for carrying families. When the automobile catches the train, an image from the private world of families (the image of the boy as innocent deriving from the Friendless One's confession) is transferred to the public world of the governor (and the train), and then is transmitted by telegraph to the prison. The climax of the movie thus represents a vast technological system which functions largely by passing images across the nation, from private sectors into public and back again. Such technology is crucial to propping up the sexuality of the private family. The movie suggests that it requires complex technological apparatuses—cars, trains, telegraphs—to convey the power of the state into the lives of private individuals and prop up ordinary men into functioning images of sexuality and fatherhood.

I suggest that the turn to technology and to the transmission of images of ordinary people at the end of this movie points to the institution of movies as having itself a crucial role in securing the sexuality of private life in the modern world. The cinema can provide for the modern world what Babylon had in the public rituals of Belshazzar. As Miriam Hansen puts it, for Griffith, Babylon is an image of "concrete utopia of a cinema that would develop, uninhibited by studio accountants and moral arbiters, into a public medium for the organization and communication of experience."[6] Hansen finds the key to Griffith's utopic cinema in the notion that cinema is a universal language, but what the movie shows Babylon as providing are crowd pleasures of sexuality, dancing, and feasting. If Babylon is an image of the utopia which cinema can provide, then what Griffith wants movies to do is to restore public rituals for satisfying desires, and thereby escape the trap of the individualist social system which removes the public as a locus of sexual satisfaction outside of marriage. The restriction of sexuality and pleasure to private life makes it too difficult to deal with the inevitable misfits: there has to be some public "outlet" for people when private life fails. Jesus and the movies are public rituals of love, according to Griffith, providing both the father figure and the public sexuality that surrounded Belshazzar.

Clearly Griffith's vision in *Intolerance* is permeated with sexist bias: he is trying to find a way to restore male power in the face of a felt threat of females who think for themselves; the movie can easily be read as a backlash against the Suffrage movement. But the sexism in this movie, like the racism in *The Birth of a Nation*, should not cause us to ignore the influence of Griffith's vision of the role of movies in the twentieth century as individualism is challenged by mass movements and mass emotions. Griffith's histories imply that private life, the supposed basis of individualism, cannot maintain itself without quite substantial social institutions which shape desires across a whole nation all at once. The movies become an important part of the system of such social institutions, partly as a way to construct desires so that they seek the "proper" objects and partly as a public ritual that allows release of emotions *not* satisfied by private life. That Griffith codes the dangerous emotions as female and cross-racial sexual desires clearly calls for ethical condemnation of his movies. But it is important nonetheless to see that what he is proposing has become the basis for the way nearly all Hollywood presents vast social issues—in terms of the strangely public sexual desires they create. Griffith also sets out the "solution" Hollywood movies will endlessly rehearse for ending the problems created by violent mass movements—the channeling of public passions either into experiences of "entertainment"—into movie-watching—or into acting out in private life roles projected from public sources. Hollywood movies after Griffith understand themselves as functioning in the interstices between private life and public social structure, and they operate by merging public and private experiences of sexuality. Griffith's movies imply that historical changes have produced the need for such public institutions shaping sexuality in order to keep sexuality from being funneled into violent mass movements which would tear the nation apart. Griffith's history is quite bizarre, but his belief in the relationship between public and private passions—between violent mass movements and sexuality—has become a commonplace of Hollywood filmmaking. This structure has provided the basis for all the most popular Hollywood love stories, as we will see in the next chapter.

3

THE PASSION OF MASS POLITICS IN THE MOST POPULAR LOVE STORIES

*H*ollywood has discovered a rather surprising sales strategy: to make popular love stories, it must surround the lovers with huge crowds pursuing political goals, and generally those goals are collectivist. For some strange reason, communism and fascism help sell love stories. Consider the four most popular love stories as calculated by constant dollars: *Gone with the Wind*, *Titanic*, *The Sound of Music*, and *Doctor Zhivago*.[1] Two of these movies—*Doctor Zhivago* and *The Sound of Music*—set their love stories against the backdrop of the violent emergence of communism and fascism. *Titanic* also uses Marxism as its backdrop; the movie takes class war as one of its themes and is set just before the Russian Revolution. James Cameron, the director, even described the movie as "holding just short of Marxist dogma."[2] The one movie in this quartet that does not focus on modern collectivism—*Gone with the Wind*—focuses on the largest mass division ever to appear within the United States, the split of the North and South over racial issues. We could add as another example of this mixture of vast political movements and private love affairs the movie that Ray Merlock called the most "popular film of the century," *Casablanca*, though it did not actually sell as well as the others.[3] This list shows that it is a formula for movie popularity to set a love story against scenes of passionate masses.

Of course these movies have powerful, deep characters, sexual tensions, and all sorts of psychoanalytic issues; nonetheless, much of their popularity and emotional impact is due to scenes in which the main characters are reduced to dots or small silhouettes against masses of people or vast landscapes that mock the importance of private life: the burning of Atlanta and Tara at sunset; a huge ship and hundreds of bodies in the water; the mountain meadows and Nazis marching; the Russian Revolution and snow-covered steppes; the Nazi invasion of France. The audiences at these movies feel not only sexuality but also the awfulness of vast powers that can move huge numbers of people about regardless of how those people feel. Rosemary Welsh notes this contradiction in *Gone with the Wind* when she says it "moves between two polarities of structure, the immediacy and intimacy of the close-up shots and the long, panoramic view of the cosmological-eye view or what has been called the God's eye view."[4]

It might seem that the vast social upheavals in these movies simply add piquancy by interrupting the love stories, thereby making the love seem all the greater for emerging in such turbulent times. But if we examine these movies carefully, we see that the turbulence parallels, supports, and often directly causes the love affairs. The passions of the masses swirling around the main characters mirror the sexual passions between them. Scarlett and Rhett are entrepreneurial personalities whose stubborn individualism mirrors the spirit brought into the Old South by the invading Northerners. The Civil War brings Scarlett and Rhett together by killing her husbands and bringing her into Rhett's arms. Similarly, the Russian Revolution brings together Zhivago and Laura, separating them from their marriages. Captain Von Trapp in *The Sound of Music* would never have realized the rigidity of his life and the lack of "love" in it if Nazism had not emerged as the grotesquely exaggerated form of his militarism.

These connections between social events and love affairs are not just odd coincidences: the emotions underlying the vast social disruptions—the political desires motivating huge mass movements—are presented as nearly identical to the emotions, the desires, leading to the love affairs. In *Titanic*, the desire to escape class oppression, which structures the crowd scenes, is directly paralleled to the emotions Rose develops upon meeting Jack: she breaks through oppressive class boundaries by leaping into Jack's arms, carrying out the desire that fuels the anger of all those people trapped below ship. The movie ends on the line that he "freed her in every way": their love somehow embodies the desire for class liberation, which is everywhere in the movie as a political theme. Similarly, in *Doctor Zhivago*, the desire to escape class oppression and unfair authority, which motivates the revolution, also seems to underlie Laura's move into Zhivago's arms. Before the revolution, Laura is impoverished and as a result manipulated and used by a wicked rich man, Komarovsky. She is quite directly rescued by the revolution, marrying the leader of the workers, Pasha. But then Pasha abandons her to become Strelnikov, a figure modeled on Stalin. When she finally finds Zhivago and a satisfying love, she is thus rescued from both her initial class oppression and the authoritarian spirit of the misguided revolution. Love is a better solution to social oppression than revolution. Or at least it is for a while. The final sadness of the movie is that Komarovsky gets her back, a plot twist that in effect converts love back into a desire for revolution: to allow the love that seemed so wonderful in this movie, we still need to get rid of the manipulative capitalists, the Komarovskys, hopefully with better leaders than Pasha/Strelnikov. *Gone with the Wind* focuses on an earlier shift in mass social formations than presented in these other movies, tracing the emergence of capitalism itself out of aristocracy, when coarse, entrepreneurial Northern carpetbaggers destroyed the graceful charm of the Old South.[5] Once again, the emotional course of the love affair *requires* this social transformation: most of the narrative of the love story is taken up with Scarlett's learning to give up her dream of the Old South, embodied in Ashley, and love instead the manipulative, entrepreneurial Rhett. As Louis Rubin Jr. puts it, "The debacle of war and the breakdown of the old plantation society serve to liberate Scarlett."[6] The movie ends rather as *Doctor Zhivago* does, with love disappearing and in a sense being converted back into a desire for a repeat of the original social upheaval: Rhett leaves Scarlett, saying that he goes off to recover the charm of the Old South, and we are left hoping somewhat ambivalently for the destruction of whatever remains of the Old South, so that Rhett will recognize that he prefers the new social order and return to loving the manipulative, entrepreneurial Scarlett.

Psychoanalytic theory could say that the intermingling of sexual and political stories in these movies shows that sex underlies everything. I propose that these movies are based on exactly the opposite premise, on the belief that the most powerful and romantic sexual desires can emerge out of—may even need to emerge out of—radical political desires such as the desire for freedom from class restrictions or the desire to destroy the whole social order.

To demonstrate that sexual emotions are represented in these movies as transformed versions of prior political or crowd emotions, I want to focus on a peculiar kind of moment which appears in each of these movies: a moment when a vast crowd scene substitutes for and becomes the representation of sexual passion, so that we in the audience are looking at and reacting to a long shot of political significance just when we were expecting to react sexually. For example, in *Casablanca*, Ilsa, having just learned that her husband is alive, leans toward Rick after he asks her about her past and replies, "Only one answer can take care of all our questions," and the image of the two lovers dissolves into a brief montage of rubble, tanks, soldiers, and planes—explosive disasters that mirror the explosive sexuality between the two of them (figs. 6 and 7).

And then a bit later, as the two embrace, we hear a muffled explosion and Ilsa asks, "Is that cannon fire or my heart pounding?" War and sexuality cannot be told apart.

Doctor Zhivago, Titanic, and *Gone with the Wind* contain similar moments when sexuality occurs offstage while we directly see violent crowd scenes or long shots which strangely resonate as images of the unrepresented sexual passion. In *Doctor Zhivago,* when Laura loses her virginity to Komarovsky, the scene is played out as a complete parallel to the passions inciting the revolution: Komarovsky leans over, kisses Laura aggressively, and the camera pulls back from their cart to linger on a military figure who turns to his men to command them "mount." There is a sudden cut to a man's crotch landing on a horse, then a gradual expansion of the shot so that we see many men mounting their horses and riding into the streets to confront the revolutionary workers. The captain commands the men to draw their sabers, and we watch the soldiers slash up marching workers, in a chaotic scene that ends with the camera moving in on Zhivago as he looks down at a patch of blood on the snow, then cutting to Laura pulling her clothes back together. Komarovsky's act of seducing Laura's virginity is thus replaced by soldiers massacring revolutionary workers. The parallel continues as Laura's fiancé, leader of the march, gives her a gun to hide, saying that from then on the revolution will no longer be peaceful (the workers have lost their innocence by shedding their blood on the snow). But the gun transfers its revolutionary violence to Laura, who ends up using it to shoot Komarovsky. Sexual and political passions are somehow interchangeable, and all concern about the condition of the poor suffering people of Russia is transferred to our concern about who is going to take care of Laura. Zhivago's great romance with her involves his violating his proper upper-class marriage, so in effect he enacts the Russian Revolution in his private life.

In *Titanic* and *Gone with the Wind,* sexuality peaks offstage while we watch images which are paralleled to scenes of mass destruction. In *Titanic,* the sexual climax occurs behind a steamed auto window, and is represented by a rather ghostly white hand that appears above the cloudy part of the window, smacks the glass, and then slides down (fig. 8). We know that the hand is only a metonymic image of the powerful movements of sexuality occurring just below that wet surface. Soon after that

Figs. 6–7. "Only one answer can take care of all our questions." ...

Destruction.

Figs. 8–9. Parallel Images: Ghostly white objects suddenly appearing.

scene, we see the ghostly white iceberg rising out of the water (fig. 9), but this time the camera descends to actually show us the explosive contact below the watery surface, and immediately after the crash the film cuts to the lovers locked in a passionate kiss.

In *Gone with the Wind*, the fiery sexual coupling of Rhett and Scarlett takes place in the dark after Rhett carries Scarlett upstairs, but in another scene we see Rhett carry Scarlett at night in front of a wall of fire as they escape Atlanta. Both scenes are structured to place the two lovers against a backdrop of a red triangle cut by stair-stepped horizontal lines: the burning buildings and the staircase alike are the locus of fiery explosive feelings (figs. 10 and 11). I suggest that we feel the heat of their relationship in that fire. The war is sexual; sexuality is warlike.

In all these movies, the explosive climaxes of the public stories—the destruction of the ship, the burning of Atlanta, the Nazi invasion, the Russian Revolution—become metaphoric representations of sexuality bursting forth. Part of the reason for these substitutions for sexuality is, of course, the Hays Code, which dictated that sexuality must be left off the screen. But censorship led to a discovery that Hollywood has clearly followed long after the Hays Code disappeared: the crowds that flock to love stories grow much larger if scenes of crowd passions provide visual substitutes for sexuality. Movie sexuality has its greatest effect on the masses if it carries with it the emotions generated from vast social upheavals.

In the G-rated family movie, *The Sound of Music*, instead of explosions substituting for sexual climaxes, we have musical numbers substituting for both explosions (which are reduced to thunder behind the song "My Favorite Things") and sexual climaxes. This movie traces a liberation from rigid, inhibiting institutions (the convent, the military) to a sexual relationship, but in this case what identifies liberation is the eruption of music. The inhibiting institutions destroy music either through enforced silence or shrill commanding whistles; liberation, both sexual and political, is identified by happy singing. The climax of this movie is a giant crowd scene in which the triumph of love and of anti-Nazi politics is represented by showing an audience undergoing the same transformation, overcoming their fear of authority to sing "Edelweiss" while surrounded by Nazi officers, after which the central couple disappears as they achieve their musical peak (winning the folk contest) and their political peak, escaping Nazi authority to the mountains.

What unites all these most popular love stories is that sexuality peaks in the dissolution of the individual, replaced by a moving crowd—

Figs. 10–11. Parallel images: Rhett carrying Scarlett across stepped red triangles.

exploding, marching, or singing. Sexuality in these movies is not represented as something private but rather is conveyed to the audience as an
experience of merging with others, losing bodily boundaries, losing control, feeling a "mass movement" so powerful that it seems to carry with
it huge crowds of people.

I am not simply punning on the word "movement": these movies
create sexuality by drawing on the political feelings that underlie actual
mass movements, the political anger about social crises affecting millions.
Hollywood relies on the emotions that threaten to fuel mass rejection of
capitalism—anger at class or gender or racial inequities—but turns those
emotions into mass support for American individualism by showing that
they would be dangerously misdirected if they became the motives for
crowd action. Instead movies construct private plots which parallel the
plots underlying public issues and hence can borrow the passions generated by those issues. Private life in twentieth-century America is no
longer conceived of as a place to escape mass emotions; it has become
instead a receptacle into which the intensity of mass emotions can be
poured without danger of riot or revolution.

In order for private life to function as the receptacle for mass emotions, the private lives of all the separate individuals in the country have
to be in some sense prepared, and that means that there need to be
social institutions which in effect model or even create private life. These
movies all represent versions of such institutions. The most important
one, of course, is the entertainment industry, which provides endless
repetitions of the story of how love develops and how private lives—
families—ought to be. *The Sound of Music* traces the development of the
new institution of public entertainment as a transformation of the family
itself. The movie starts by showing a world divided rigidly into institutions all devoid of entertainment: the military, the convent, the aristocratic family house, which we first see structured very much on the
model of the others, with the captain using a whistle to order people
about. Maria represents the agent of change that alters the rigidity of
these institutions, by in effect bringing the power of music into the convent and then into the family. In the convent she seems just a disturbance,
something that does not fit, but in the family she becomes the catalyst
for a radical change that expands the aristocratic house into an essential
part of the system of mass entertainment.

The first thing she does is produce clothing designed to allow the
children to have "fun" and she does so by reshaping drapes and other
accouterments of the house. The shift from stately drapes to fun clothes

is a change in structure that marks the beginning of the transformation of the family into an institution intertwined with mass entertainment. The captain steadfastly resists, then accepts, each step in this transformation. First he accepts the clothing of the children, then he accepts music itself, joining in performances at home, and then he takes the final and most important step, allowing his family to perform in public.

The family is transformed into a public entity through a series of performances for a gradually increasing audience. First, there is a "private" show just for family members—the goatherder song—and what is performed in that show is the story of the formation of a family in a setting devoid of any social group at all, a boy and a girl meeting in the mountains. Then there is the goodbye song sung to a large party of people at their house. This second performance shows the house itself being divided into public and private spaces: the song marks the separation as the children each say goodbye in a distinctive musical way and then retreat from the public setting into the private spaces of the bedrooms. This is the first public performance of privacy. As part of this gathering, we also have the performance of the Linzer Waltz by the captain and Maria, on the terrace, slightly removed from the rest of the guests who are dancing inside: by dancing, the couple are both falling in love, moving towards their own private space, and also, at the same time, finding that they can fit beautifully into the social order: their private love moves lockstep with a public ritual.

The final performance is of course at the folk festival, when the captain allows the family to be completely public. Just before this final, most public performance, the movie includes its one brief long shot of Nazis gathering—troops marching across a square—and this shot sets up the festival performance as an alternative to marching as a way of organizing crowds. As the family's performance approaches during the festival, we see Nazis stationing themselves throughout the room to entrap the family, so the act of transforming the family into a public institution seems at first to threaten the destruction of the family. Instead, this particular move of uniting the family with public presentation, with a role in mass society, results in their escape from the Nazis. The crowd functions here to defend the family rather than to destroy it, and it functions that way precisely because the family wins the contest: the crowd is in effect protecting its own pleasure, its entertainment. The last song further identifies the performing family with the spirit of the crowd, as the captain leads the audience in singing "Edelweiss." He says that this song is his goodbye song, in what seems a repetition of the earlier goodbye song of the children; he would seem to be retreating into the Nazi military machine.

Instead, he is preparing to leave the military entirely for a life as part of a performing family, running an inn in Vermont as the singing Von Trapps.

The captain's last song, "Edelweiss," functions to create the audience for his future performances, by asserting the value of entertainment over the value of militarism. The song is an act of resistance because it is somehow purely Austrian and hence resists the German takeover. But equally important is that the song identifies the nation with a delicate flower, something that cannot be militarized and which is aligned with beauty, pleasure, and consumption rather than disciplined goal-seeking. Furthermore, the song is also identified with the love that creates the perfect family: it first appears in the movie when the captain hears Maria singing it with the children, and he says, "You've brought music back into the house"—an allusion to what they used to do with his wife before she died. This is of course a hint that Maria will be the next wife, but more, it identifies the song with the notion of the perfect family— one that is devoted to the pleasures of beauty. The song thus serves in this movie both to create the loving family and to create the mass that can resist Nazism: this mass is precisely the Hollywood audience that is devoted to love, pleasure, and entertainment rather than marching for a cause. When the captain brings the audience to sing this song he is in effect bringing music (and by extension, sexuality, pleasure, consumerism, and the whole world of private pleasures) into the "house" of the nation, setting the entire social order based on "love," the individualized consumerist social order, against the Nazis. The modern capitalist social order is based on mass distribution of the core of private life, on everyone being trained in the wholesome "pleasure" of family life as an alternative to the lustful passion of marching.

The final performance foreshadows the future life of this family, which moves to Vermont and runs a musical inn: the family is quite literally converted into a business which provides entertainment for the masses. Though the movie does not indicate this future, the climactic moment is their winning the folk festival, in a sense establishing their singing as of a professional nature. The movie thus reflects back on the movie industry itself, which presents what it is doing as entertainment requiring great professional expertise but used for fun and light-heartedness, not for politics—though the movie also implies that entertainment can serve political goals. The Nazis are defined essentially as persons who will militarize all of society, and thereby eliminate entertainment and love. This effect of Nazis is represented by Rolf, who first sings a love song to the daughter, then, after becoming a Nazi, stops his courting and is finally seen blowing a whistle to turn the family in to the Nazis and stop their escape: Rolf moves in the opposite direction from the captain, going from music (entertainment) to whistles (militarism).

There is a fairly obvious irony in the family beating the Nazis by winning a "folk festival": Hitler identifies Nazism as the "folkish state," and defines its goal in terms that resonate with the effort to promote folkish arts: "the highest purpose of a folkish state is concern for the preservation of those original racial elements which bestow culture and create the beauty and dignity of a higher mankind."[7] The movie presents the Von Trapp family as bestowing culture and creating beauty for the "folk," while the Nazis would, the movie implies, destroy the folk arts. Even the racial goal of Nazism seems in part hinted at in the song the captain sings: Edelweiss, a white flower, represents the essential cultural core of Austria, and identifying that core so much with whiteness (especially in an American movie), hints at racial identification. The contrast between the Von Trapps and the Nazis is obviously not presented as "racially" defined—everyone is white—but one can say that what is presented is a contest about which of these ways of expressing the essential whiteness, or racial, folk core of the people is the truest—singing or militarizing the nation?

The "escape" of this family from the Nazis invokes the transformation of rigid discipline and rigid class structures (such as the distinction between the baroness Eberfeld and the governess Maria) into a seemingly classless consumerist society. Even the nuns join in breaking out of their morally structured life to help this family, saying to their superior, "We have sinned" in stealing auto parts from the Nazis' cars. Those acts are exceptional breaks with usual morality due to the presence of genuine evil, but they also resonate with the general loosening of morality and its replacement with an ethos of love and entertainment. Throughout the movie, "loosening up" has been identified as good, and following any strict rule (even that of being very well dressed) is identified as bad.

In *Casablanca*, as well, entertainment is a locus of resistance to political oppression. Rick's Café Americain is an oasis of American entertainment within the world of European political movements, so that Rick's decision to leave his café would seem an image of the movement out of the world of entertainment (the world Hollywood insists its movies create) into the world of politics, and his disappearance into the fog is not only an end of this movie but, temporarily, an end of the world of movies. However, the film shows repeatedly that the everyday running of the world of entertainment is permeated by political issues. One of Rick's first gestures is to exclude a man who is identified as a Nazi, and later Rick rigs a roulette game to allow a young woman to escape having to sleep with Renault to get a pass out of Casablanca. These two examples suggest that the details of running an entertainment institution (whom to allow in, how to deal with money) lead to political decisions. The central plot issue—Rick's hiding and then using papers which would allow anyone to escape the Nazis—shows his willingness to risk political dangers.

But it is not simply in behind-the-scenes acts that Rick uses his business to engage with political issues. The very entertainment he presents invokes themes that are close to political issues of great importance without naming them. Consider Sam's presence: in the context of Nazi rule, the question of race hangs in the air, though never mentioned in the dialogue itself. In Sam's second song, though, he draws attention to his race, singing, "Though my hair is curly . . . though my teeth are pearly." The word "though" suggests that the song will end up saying that Sam is not going to be excluded "though" he is different physically than others. We don't hear the end of this song, but it seems to say that Sam can do whatever anyone else can do, even though he is black. And the most important act Sam performs in this context is to entertain, to create pleasure, and thus to facilitate love. The question of the roles of blacks in this movie arises not only because of Nazi racism, but because the movie is set in Casablanca, in Africa; the movie trades on an escape route from Europe to the United States that involves going through the "dark continent." So Sam's presence invokes several political issues: racial exclusion of Nazis, and the relation of Africa to Europe and the United States. The United States represents freedom in this movie, and a crucial part of that freedom, the movie implies, is racial freedom. The racial issues in U.S. history are invoked when Rick says, "I don't buy and sell human beings," as a response to Ferrari's offer of money to hire Sam. Further, when Rick tells of the day the Nazis entered Paris, he remembers it as a contrast between Ilsa and the Nazis: "The Germans wore gray, you wore blue"; perhaps it is a stretch to identify blue and gray as Civil War colors, but in the context of a movie that invokes issues of slavery and racism and the contrast between the United States and Germany, the Civil War stands behind the whole thematics of the film: Germany needs a civil war to escape its racial problem as the United States did.

The role of entertainment as political statement becomes central in the main plot when we see the one act that reveals the power of Lazlo: he gets the people in the café to sing *La Marseillaise* to drown out a

German song. The movie shows the people in the café inspired by this song, even though quite a few of those who are so inspired are not French. The song seems to be one of freedom far more than nationalism. And a crucial detail of Lazlo's success is that he needs Rick to nod his head to the band to get them to play the song: Rick, as mogul of this entertainment institution, chooses to allow a political form of entertainment. The result of this song, however, is that the Nazis then shut down Rick's café, an image of what would happen if entertainment too overtly confronted political leaders. The movie suggests that it cannot get too close in its own entertainment to real political issues. Thus, when saloon-keeper Rick finally decides to join the anti-Nazi movement, he does not simply turn his form of entertainment into politics; rather, he sells the café first, seemingly keeping entertainment and politics separate.

The final decision Rick makes, to send Ilsa with Lazlo, thus looks like a straightforward choice of a social goal over his private life and a choice of politics over entertainment. As he says, "The problems of three little people don't amount to a hill of beans in this crazy world." But the imagery on the screen does not show us three little people as tiny "beans" in a huge world: rather we see intense closeups of Ilsa and Rick and Lazlo, three gigantic heads that visually contradict Rick's words. As Rick says that his private life does not matter anymore, it is his private life that we care about most intensely, and it is our feelings about Rick's private life that the movie uses to persuade us to join a mass movement. (The film clearly aims to bring viewers to support the U.S.'s entering the war against Germany.) Rick also says that while he and Ilsa are separating, they now have Paris, which is important, because it implies that the reason they can join the war effort is that they have recovered their love. When he believed he had lost that love, when she disappeared in Paris, he became a cynical, self-centered person. So this ending does not finally suggest that Rick gives up personal relationships to join a mass movement, but rather that his deep investment in a personal relationship leads him to join the mass effort. The choice between personal and public goals is not coded as a choice between individual and mass, but rather a choice between cynical isolationism and selfless love. In other words, all the emotions that we say are part of the personal, intimate sphere are the very emotions which tie Rick to mass spheres: the personal is transubstantiated into the social, the mass.[8]

Rick actually fuels the anti-Nazi movement in this movie by transferring his private love into a public image of love which can then be shared worldwide. Let me explain. Helping Lazlo is not directly helping the military battle against Hitler because Lazlo does not physically fight the Nazis; rather he creates publicity, running newspapers, to drum up sentiment against them. He is a figurehead, a star; freeing Lazlo from Nazi control is a contribution to the media industry. Rick does that but also does much more than simply free Lazlo from constraint: he also essentially gives Ilsa to Lazlo because she is, Rick says, "the thing which keeps him going." Apparently, for Lazlo to be a successful media figure around which people will gather, he needs to have Ilsa. Rick's words could mean that Lazlo needs Ilsa to provide a private life to keep Lazlo's spirits up, but what the movie implies is that Ilsa is actually necessary to shape the media images Lazlo projects. Her going with him adds a distinct aura to him as an image on the screen. Rick is thus giving Lazlo not merely a private life but also a public image of masculinity and sexual passion, the image of the perfect couple, of ideal love. It is this quality which Hollywood sets against Nazism; it is the public image of the idealism of love that the movie presents as the essence of anti-Nazism (or, we might say, it is what Hollywood movies believe they can contribute to anti-Nazism).

While the movie thus ends up representing love as the antidote to Nazism, it does so only by converting love into a fraudulent image of itself. The movie seems to expose the tenuous logic of Hollywood individualism, that Hays Code logic which says that movies can use the power of mass images to promulgate private morality even as the distribution of those images inherently destroys private morality. In this movie, Rick constructs an image of the perfect moral private life—an image of marriage—at the same time that he demonstrates the image is false. Ilsa and Rick clearly love each other, yet the movie concludes that her real sexual passion, her love, is less important than the false images of love she can create to help out the anti-Nazi movement. There are two such images, one for Lazlo in private, as she and Rick conspire to convince Lazlo that she loves him, and one for the public, as the world audience (and the theater audience) sees her as a noble figure precisely for sleeping with a man she does not love. Her leaving with Lazlo pours the passion she feels with Rick into a publicity campaign, and this is the fundamental logic of this movie, to bring people to want to join the American war effort as a result of their desire for Ilsa (and by extension, their desire for pleasure, for Paris, for movies, for entertainment). The image that leads people to join the mass movement of anti-Nazism is an image of an idealized couple, not an image of any oppressed masses at all. Similarly, Rick's leaving with Renault to join the Resistance is not seen in terms of their dissolving into a mass of soldiers; rather it is seen as two men walking along speaking of "the beginning of a beautiful friendship."

The movie ends thus with two images of idealized couples, beautiful private relationships, as the essence of the anti-Nazi movement—but not private couples going off to live in private; rather private couples going off to become public images and parts of public movements. I suggest that Ilsa and Lazlo go off rather as the captain and Maria go off—to become public performers of love as part of media industries, entertainment industries, and it is this that answers the challenge of collectivism.

As for *Gone with the Wind*, the whole movie is about one set of social institutions, the New South, replacing another set, the Old South. Both institutions are defined by kinds of pleasures and private lives. Ashley's plantation had "charm and grace," and the "high soft laughter of Negroes," as if what Ashley did in running it was put on shows for the Negroes, shows that were "soft" and gentle, or we might say, genteel—aristocratic entertainment. The new institution provides a different kind of pleasure, identified with the violent passions which course through Rhett and Scarlett's love affair. Hence the image of the new relation of master and slave is Rhett's giving a red (or should we say "scarlet"?) petticoat to Mammy: instead of the soft laughter Ashley claimed to provide his slaves, Rhett will provide the intense pleasures of sexuality and exciting fashion. A new mass-produced sexuality (e.g., red petticoats) replaces the rigid relationships of slavery; the New South is the movies, the Old South the minuet.

These passions of the New South derive from the destructive violence of the Northern invasion, which unleashes new productive forces that are identified with the sexuality of the main couple. That is why, as I suggested earlier, the rape of Atlanta is paralleled by Rhett's rape of Scarlett (in two red triangles, like the red triangle of Mammy's petticoat). Rhett's rape of Scarlett reveals to her the pleasures of sexuality and of manipulation, similar to the pleasures she finds in aggressively running her companies; the rape of the South reveals to the South the pleasures of industry and entrepreneurial energy as better than the decaying economy of slavery. Scarlett uses her beauty to restore the beauty of Tara, and this use of sexual energy is what fuels the new social order. What seems the private pleasure of sexuality is also then a vast set of public institutions, which fuel the New South.

I am suggesting a similarity in the sense of "new institutions" emerging in *Gone with the Wind*, *The Sound of Music*, and *Casablanca*: the new entrepreunerial South, the performing family, and Lazlo's publicity machine all publicize and mass-produce sexuality and love. I want to suggest similar effects in *Doctor Zhivago* and *Titanic*. In these two movies, though, there is a difference: the new institutions are rather mechanical and uninspiring, and so need to be "enlivened" by the recovery of the spirit of the moment of change, the moment when an old order fell apart. These movies add in an element, which we have not yet discussed, to the Hollywood presentation of institutions of entertainment: the need for a kind of permanent revolution, a permanent battle against oppression, to fire the passions that keep sexuality and private life burning.

In the film *Titanic*, the change of institutions is represented by the difference between the two huge ships we see: the *Titanic* and the salvage vessel. The Titanic is structured as an institution of oppression based on rigid divisions between classes and genders. The salvage ship is presented as a much more egalitarian structure, in which there is no clear distinction between leaders and workers nor between male and female: everyone wears jeans and everyone seems to have expertise and abilities. But this new ship is seeking something from the old ship, something the new ship lacks, and what that turns out to be is on the surface a love that transcends material dimensions. But what we see being recovered is not simply love, but a passion that fights against restrictions. It is Rose herself who is finally recovered from the sunken ship, from the other era, and it is her spirit that the new ship needs, the spirit of revolution.

The parallels between Rose, the structure of the ship, and the structure of society in general run throughout the movie. The parallels between Rose and the ship start when she begins her story, saying, "Inside, I was screaming" and the film cuts to the ship's whistle blowing, as if the ship too was screaming. That the iceberg's penetration of the ship later parallels her sexual intercourse with Jack simply continues an extended analogy that structures the entire story. She starts off contemplating suicide, and she finally commits a kind of suicide in destroying her old, class- and gender-based self; the ship also commits a kind of suicide, plunging onto the iceberg as a way of being eventually replaced by the new, classless ship.

Much of Rose's "escape" from her old life is portrayed as an escape from parts of the ship and a transformation of the ship. Her first image of an alternative life is created by standing with Jack on the prow with their hands out—riding the ship in a way other than sitting properly in their rooms. Her efforts to escape her old life become a series of efforts to

escape the lower decks, involving escaping both the overall imprison-
ment of the lower classes by the ship's authorities and the particular im-
prisonment of Jack by her fiancé Cal's private police force, his servant
with a gun. She cuts open Jack's handcuffs as part of the plot of their
love affair; later they force open a metal door between decks, as part of
the general effort of the lower decks to escape. These paralleled acts of
removing barriers between classes lead to the ultimately classless ship that
replaces the *Titanic*.

When Rose recounts her life after losing Jack, she describes working
and marrying and ending up solidly middle-class—this is the capitalist
image of classlessness, merging the upper and lower in a universal middle.
Her final gesture, throwing the diamond overboard, presents itself as
evidence of her complete liberation from upper-class values; Patrick
McGee sees this gesture as the most completely revolutionary act in the
movie, going beyond the entire system of capitalism and beyond all materialist revolts against capitalism, transcending all concern with "capital
value" to find the "incommensurable" that is the "true goal of life."[9] I
suggest rather that it is part of the transfer of revolutionary spirit from
materialist mass action to the code of love. What Rose values after Jack
is coded as something that cannot have generic value to everyone, cannot
be measured or converted to money: it is the basis of value (love) rather
than a means of acquiring a value that can be derived from others (as any
valuable object or skill could be). This transformation is also what the
outer story of the movie performs: a training of the materialist scientists
in a system of personal values that transforms them. What has to be
recovered from the sunken ship, from the wreckage of the old social
order, is passion, not a gem. And that passion is both the passion of a
love that transcends material bounds and the passion of class anger, of
revolution.

There is a strange way in which technology itself is presented in this
movie as the mechanism for making the experience of revolution a permanent system by transforming that experience into the endlessly repeat-
able experiences of being entertained, getting angry at oppression, falling
in love, and mixing all those emotions together. There are two technolo-
gies in the movie: the technology of the salvage ship and the technology
of the movie itself. The technology of the movie is highlighted repeatedly in transitions that are clearly technologically mediated: from the
photographs at the beginning to the recreated ship; from the ruins in the
water to the recreated reality of the Victorian world; and finally, from
Rose's deathbed to the "afterlife" ballroom scene. Rose teaches the salvage crew that they should be excavating love, not jewels, and the movie

teaches its viewers that the vast technological system of the movie industry is also devoted to promulgating and maintaining love. But what love is, according to this movie, is a permanent possibility of escaping social oppression, a permanent experience of revolution. The problem in the 1990s is, bizarrely enough, the feeling that there is no oppression to fight (perhaps because the communist threat is gone): the movie has to go back and recover an old oppression to revive passion.

Rose is "freed in all ways" and this is what the movie tries to do for us. To be freed, one needs the experience first of being restricted, oppressed: to make falling in love such an act of freeing, there must first be the feeling of economic or political oppression to generate the desire for liberation; the movies require then the political/economic oppression to generate the passion that then can be freed from all connection to political/economic structures in the form of "love."

In *Doctor Zhivago*, as in *Titanic*, the old structure of upper and lower classes, of fancy balls and poverty-stricken laborers, is gone, replaced by technology: *Zhivago* ends on the image of a dam. A dam channels great energy and movement, so the movie shows that at least the revolution does still embody the "movement" which gave birth to it. But the dam seems utterly unmoved by the passionate flow going through it: like Yuri's brother Yevgraf, it has lost the passion that created it. Ending oppressive divisions within society in both these movies seems to result in a technological order, equalizing everyone as cogs. The two movies are both narrated as flashbacks from a modern technological scene back to the moment when the older order exploded, the moment of revolution. Both movies show new kinds of leaders who seem at first heartless materialists or technocrats, but eventually are revealed as deeply in need of the passion they uncover in the past—General Yevgraf on the dam and Brock Lovett at the helm of the salvage ship. The very passion that destroyed the old structures, the passion of revolution, is what is needed to make the powerful new structures worth having.

In *Doctor Zhivago*, what condemns the revolution that started off so passionately seems to be the absence of sexual desire and private life: it is a purely material revolution (as the salvage ship seems to be motivated by purely material goals). Pasha, the first "leader" of the revolution we meet, defines himself as having no "amorous experience"; once installed into power, he declares that the "personal life is dead." The frame tale of General Yevgraf, who has succeeded in the revolution, shows him depressed and passionless; he says he isn't "any kind of an uncle" and, lacking love, is clearly searching for the love his brother found, but doesn't know how to find it—he wants the passion that turned into mechanical order, the surging tide passing through the dam, not the dam itself.

Yuri Zhivago had passion: love, poetry, and, apparently, through his genes, the "gift" of balalaika-playing (which seems only to be given to women). Where is passion and balalaika-playing in a dam-structured society? The water pouring over the dam at the very end of the movie, raising a rainbow, seems to be an image of beauty and even of passion, of that flow which cannot be ever encapsulated in stone or perfectly planned. But to have the spirit of the surging masses of water is to have the spirit of the revolution permanently and that, this movie implies, is to have the spirit of love. The huge technological marvels that are the salvage ship in *Titanic* and the dam at the end of *Doctor Zhivago* are beautiful, but need the central passion inside them, so that the power and energy they produce will be leashed to driving passions for the society. We might say both have to find a relationship to the vast water around them. Lovett wants to extract the gem from the ocean and have nothing to do with the power of water which ultimately caused the destruction of the original ship. Similarly, Yevgraf as director of the dam wants to extract power and channel it precisely: but this extraction of material power from the vast tide ignores the passion that is defined as the moving force that allows this wealth to be available. What unlocks wealth and power in these movies is passion.

When Zhivago and Lara find their passion, they do so in structures that seem removed from the center of society, in a temporary apartment or a big house utterly separated from all the rest of the social order—without any deliveries or public services supporting it. Their relationship is presented as something standing outside the social order, but not simply disconnected from everything else: rather they become the embodiment of the resistance to the old social order, and hence the spirit of the new, the spirit the revolutionaries should have been seeking, just as Rhett and Scarlett are the spirit of the New South. Hollywood movies rely on moments when the social order is undergoing such upheaval to create a kind of love that can seem to stand against society and yet be supported by mass desires at the same time. Hollywood needs moments of oppression and revolution to fuel the passion that can be seen as great love worthy of the support of vast audiences who watch the movies, and that is what these most popular movies show. This is why *Titanic* had to resurrect the Marxist moment of class war to create the plot that would produce the love it wanted to present.

The movies thus borrow the anger and desire for liberation which fuel movements against social injustice, and find in those emotions a desire that turns easily into love and thereby produces the feeling of liberation—very much as a pure feeling, a joy, not a change in political or economic state. Yet this sidetracking covers up or ignores the group being oppressed in the first place. In each of these movies there is an unnamed other group that is really the main target of the oppressions being fought against. We watch instead what could be called a "screen scene" of oppression whereby a few characters in the dominant group suffer unfairly: Hence we watch the threatened oppression of a wealthy white Austrian family rather than Jews in *The Sound of Music*; the oppression of the rich white Scarlett jammed into a corset rather than blacks in *Gone with the Wind*; the suffering of Rick and Lazlo rather than Jews in *Casablanca*; the liberation of the declassed aristocrat Laura rather than any real workers in *Doctor Zhivago*; and the similar liberation of the impoverished aristocrat Rose as a result of her contact with someone in that class that is actually oppressed and killed by the ship—Jack, the representative of the working class. *Titanic* hints at another oppressed group left out of the story when Rose opens the story of her life by claiming that to her, the *Titanic* "was a slave ship, taking me back to America in chains." The voyage of the *Titanic* is then a version of the middle passage, and Jack's dying on the way makes him a substitute for the Africans who died en route to America. But even Jack's death ends up covering up his oppression, because he is resurrected as an aristocrat in the afterlife scene.

In none of these movies do we see any images of the oppression that really defined the evil of the old social order—no images of mistreatment of Jews or blacks or workers as part of the regular working of the oppressive system. At most, we have images of some of these persons being killed in the struggle to break free. The movies thus leave out the need to change unfair systems of power and money to achieve liberation. All that is needed is passion.

Actually, the issue of transferring money and power is treated rather ingeniously in all of these movies: the act of liberation is identified with someone in the ruling class giving up power and money. Rose's liberation is marked by her never using the Star of the Sea, so that liberation is clearly not an economic issue at all, but a purely "personal" one. Similarly, Laura and Zhivago's liberation into love is identified with their having to do housework without servants, Rick's "liberation" involves giving up his wealthy position in his club, and Captain Von Trapp gives up his wealth and goes to work in an inn. While these movies borrow the anger of those who are economically and politically oppressed, the act of escaping oppression within these films is carried out rather bizarrely by having someone rich and powerful voluntarily and happily and temporarily drop into the world of the oppressed. We could add in here another very popular movie, *Love Story,* as also carrying out this same plot: to overcome the oppression of the lower class, an oppression signified by the prejudicial attitudes of the rich boy's family toward his lower-class girlfriend, the boy gives up his wealth and earns it back through labor. These movies do strongly imply the unfairness of wealth and power as it has been distributed, but the way redistribution occurs is that a few wealthy people drop in wealth as a result of falling in love (and generally end up going to work and re-earning their wealth), but no poor or oppressed persons rise in wealth. These movies suggest that liberation is a dematerializing process, an act of being driven by passion beyond the rationality of money.

These movies present the mass desire to escape oppression as a force that changes the kinds of desires found in private life. In each of these movies, the "old" order is represented by a relationship between two persons who seem to belong together by class (the captain and the baroness, Zhivago and his first wife, Rose and her fiancé) or some kind of ethnicity (as Ilsa and Lazlo are European and speak English with accents). The historical disruption that is broadly altering class or ethnic relationships brings with it a new lover of a different class or a slightly different ethnicity (American Rick or Irish Jack), who makes the situation a triangle. Violent disruption of the social order carries with it a sexual disruption of private life. The old private life was devoted to a certain sense of propriety or morality or "normalcy": the new one is devoted to breaking free, to liberation and passion. The old love had security and familiarity; the new love has energy. To experience this new form of love, individuals are trained by Hollywood to conceive of their sexuality as a kind of permanent political revolution. These historical romances allow viewers to return to moments of mass revolution and borrow the passions generated by such moments over and over again.

4

LOVING THE CROWD: TRANSFORMATIONS OF GENDER IN EARLY SOVIET AND NAZI FILMS

*W*hile Hollywood sought methods to make crowd emotions supportive of personal emotions, filmmakers in collectivist countries—the Soviet Union and Nazi Germany in particular—experimented with ways to make life in the crowd more important, more trustworthy, and even more real than personal life. The results were films in which the presence of the crowd thoroughly eclipses moments of interpersonal conversation, films in which individuals hardly exist, and films in which elements that Hollywood firmly places in the private sphere—including sexuality and gender—are revised into public forms.

The valuing of crowd emotions over individual consciousness runs throughout communist and fascist political commentary. We can see an early version of this preference in *The Communist Manifesto* of 1857, in which Karl Marx laments what capitalism has done to the crowd passions of earlier social orders: "The bourgeoisie, wherever it has got the upper hand . . . has drowned the most heavenly ecstasies of religious fervour, of chivalrous enthusiasm, of philistine sentimentalism, in the icy water of egotistical calculation."[1]

Marx wishes to restore the "ecstasies" and "enthusiasm" that were felt before capitalism. He even sees the most virulent expression of such emotions—riots—as a crucial motivating force that will bring about the workers' revolution:

> With the development of industry the proletariat not only increases in number; it becomes concentrated in greater masses, its strength

grows, and it feels that strength more. . . . The workers begin to form combinations (Trades' Unions) against the bourgeois. . . . Here and there the contest breaks out into riots.

Now and then the workers are victorious, but only for a time. The real fruit of their battles lies, not in the immediate result, but in the ever-expanding union of the workers.[2]

Marx describes riots as bearing "fruit," which he describes as the growing feeling of strength and unity among workers. Riots are frequently invoked in accounts of crowd psychology, but Hollywood filmmakers and Marx interpret the "fruit" of riots quite differently. To Hollywood filmmakers, riots show the loss of moral resistance to suggestion; to Marx, they show the growth of a new proletariat morality.

Hitler similarly calls for the replacement of the "wavering" individual with the mass body, saying that when a person enters a

mass demonstration . . . and has thousands and thousands of people of the same opinions around him, . . . he is swept away by three or four thousand others into the mighty effect of suggestive intoxication and enthusiasm, . . . then he himself has succumbed to the magic influence of what we designate as "mass suggestion." The will, the longing, and also the power of thousands are accumulated in every individual. The man who enters such a meeting doubting and wavering leaves it inwardly reinforced: he has become a link in the community.[3]

Hitler praises just what Hollywood, in the Hays Code, feared, the magical power of "mass suggestion" to replace the "mass resistance" of individual consciousness.

Early Soviet and Nazi filmmakers sought intense emotional moments that would disrupt normal, individualist thought processes. Sergei Eisenstein aims quite directly at getting audiences carried away; he describes his films as built of "attractions," moments which are as powerfully transportive emotionally as amusement park rides. He creates powerful emotions through what he calls montage, a distinct alternative to Hollywood continuity and realism. Montage is built of sequences of images that, Eisenstein says, conflict with each other, requiring the viewer to engage in a dialectic process to find syntheses and transcend the conflicts. At the lowest level, the perception of physical movement is a synthesis of one image followed by another that is slightly different. For example, we see a man with his legs together, then the same man with his legs slightly apart. Since the two images are projected on the same space, but cannot coexist, we interpret them as "movement": the man moved his legs between the two stills. From two conflicting stills to "movement" is a small step of dialectic. Going that far, film creates a stronger reality effect than still pictures. But Eisenstein considers that small step the beginning of a dialectic that then goes beyond reality. If we can create a sense of physical "movement" from two conflicting still images, then we can create other kinds of "movement" from other kinds of conflict. For example, what he calls "emotional dynamization," or movement of emotions, arises when two intercut sequences of film have an "emotional" conflict; he gives as an example a still, quiet scene intercut with a violent one, which might not even be connected to the first "in reality."[4] More complex is his description of a three-step process leading to intellectual "movement": "*Conflict within a thesis* (an abstract idea)— *formulates* itself in the dialectics of the sub-title—*forms* itself spatially in the conflict within the shot—and *explodes* with increasing intensity in montage-conflict among the separate shots."[5] Let me give a small example of this process: in *The Battleship Potemkin*, one of the subtitles is "Of Men and Maggots," after which we see a scene in which sailors complain of the maggots in their meat. At one point, we see the sailors from very high up: they are all in white, circling around the officers in black. The shot has no clear and obvious meaning. But then there is a close-up of the maggots in the beef, which are white worms crawling all over the dark meat. The similarity between the shots of maggots and of men suggests that we have not merely been watching a reproduction of real events, but rather have been seeing quite staged arrangements. The parallel shots interact with the title to create a fairly clear double meaning: not only are the men complaining about maggots, they are being treated as maggots. But once we have passed such a moment, everything in the film becomes more than merely "real," and when a stone lion "stands up" because three different stone lions have been cut together in sequence (one lying, one crouching, one standing up), we are ready to read such an "event" as something other than "reality."

These are fairly simple examples. In *October*, Eisenstein produced a much more complex montage, as a way of commenting on a counterrevolutionary military action led by General Kornilov. Here is Eisenstein's description of the sequence in the film:

> Kornilov's march on Petrograd was under the banner of "In the Name of God and Country." Here [in the film] we attempted to

reveal the religious significance of this episode in a rationalistic way. A number of religious images, from a magnificent Baroque Christ to an Eskimo idol, were cut together. The conflict in this case was between the concept and the symbolization of God. Maintaining the denotation of "God," the images increasingly disagree with our concept of God, inevitably leading to individual conclusions about the true nature of all deities.[6]

Eisenstein thus creates a text requiring a complex method of reading based on dialectical steps, designed to create "movement" in the minds of viewers. It is not a process of establishing an ideology (through, say, defining some particular reality), but rather a process of constantly breaking through each attempt at ideological synthesis. As Eisenstein summarizes, "It is art's task to make manifest the contradictions of Being."[7] Eisenstein compares the dialectic within his movies to the historical dialectic as Lenin defines it: a process of "deepening human perception" until things no longer seem what they were (a process of "negation"), followed by a return to the "old," but transformed, way of seeing (a "negation of the negation)."[8] This is not a process of establishing a reality or an ideological synthesis, but rather of refusing to settle on any single schema of perception. Bill Nichols argues that Eisenstein's greatest contribution to cinema is his requiring the audience to recognize their involvement in constructing history, constructing reality. Nichols traces a line from Eisenstein's films to Errol Morris's *Thin Blue Line* and Oliver Stone's *JFK* in terms of movies that use various "fictionalizations" of reality in order to leave viewers with the task of constructing some new kind of reality.[9] These movies remain unstable, even years after they are made, and merely not because they disrupt the preconstructed realities of Hollywood clichés as, say, Godard movies do. Eisenstein's movies engage us in the process of interpretation, but not as independent individuals; rather, they seek to "move" us to join together in a social process of constructing meaning.

If Eisenstein rejects the construction of a stable reality and of individual characters, it should be fairly obvious that he will have trouble constructing a traditional narrative, since the basic form of such narratives is the conflict or growing union between two individuals. Eisenstein instead constructs in *Potemkin* a story of the conflict and union of collectives, represented as sets of anonymous bodies and ships. Eisenstein states quite directly his goal of developing a new form of narrative:

Discarding the individualist conception of the bourgeois hero, our films . . . made an abrupt deviation—insisting on an understanding of the mass as hero.

No screen had ever before reflected an image of collective action. Now the conception of "collectivity" was to be pictured.[10]

Eisenstein is not only stating a political goal, but also describing a narrative strategy: beginning his films with the "discarding" of what appears to be an individual hero, then passing through an "abrupt deviation" into seeing the "mass" as hero.

Consider how this works in the film *The Battleship Potemkin.* The movie begins with a conflict between oppressed sailors and evil officers during which a leader of the sailors emerges, Vakulinchuk, who brings them to open rebellion. The rebellion roughly follows Hollywood sequencing, climaxing in an individual battle between Vakulinchuk and one of the officers. However, this fight between hero and villain does not occur at the climax of the whole movie, but instead less than a third of the way through, and with a surprising result: Vakulinchuk is killed, yet the sailors' rebellion succeeds. After the battle, there is an interlude during which Vakulinchuk's body is put on display in a rough-hewn shrine in the harbor. Crowds gather to view it and various speakers emerge to encourage rebellion. The end of this sequence is a special effect: after an intertitle says, "Sunrise. There is an uprising," a dissolve makes it appear that an empty staircase is magically filled with people, all moving together upwards. This "uprising" of the people seems one with the "sunrise" and hence a natural phenomenon, a part of the turning of the earth and other vast motions. The odd thing about the movie from this point on is that no further leaders are created or identified; indeed nobody in the movie ever has a name after Vakulinchuk dies. Equally odd, the wicked officers (who also had names before the rebellion) never appear again. The fights from then on are between masses of anonymous "people" and masses of anonymous soldiers and sailors loyal to the never-again-seen officers.

What Eisenstein has staged, then, is the mutual elimination of individuals on both sides. The final confrontation pits the rebel sailors on the battleship *Potemkin* against a fleet of ships loyal to the czar. But no battle occurs; instead, after pointing cannon at each other, the two sides join together and sail off toward revolution. That joining is signaled by flags, but we never see any leaders or even any individual sailors on the czarist ships making the decision to join the rebels. We never even have a close-up of any czarist sailors. One can imagine a Hollywood version of these same events: there would be intense focus on the czarist sailors and their tough decisions, presented in terms of individual moral quandaries which would be resolved by someone becoming a leader and persuading all the rest. Instead, we have two masses of sailors agreeing to join together, filmed largely in long shots so individuals blur together into crowds.

The movie does show the persons in it experiencing strong emotions, but there is always an equation between the presentation of such emotions and images of mechanical processes. Hence, the rising anger of the men is reflected in the boiling of the soup in large bowls; the anxiety of the night before the confrontation with the czarist ships is represented by pistons pumping and arms moving repetitively. Interspersed through these mechanical processes there are numerous close-ups of individual faces, but never in small conversations that would reveal the "private" thoughts in those minds. Further, the close-ups are not structured to repeatedly come back to the same face (or to a few faces), so we never get to "know" any particular persons or their individual reactions. Eisenstein is known for his close-ups of faces, but the faces do not thereby define private interpersonal spaces: rather the faces are presented as parts of a complex process involving machines. Each face reveals an emotion that is derived not from the character of the person but from the material surroundings. The film does not collect together the emotions of one person, but rather what Marx would call the emotional "sublimate of material processes."[11]

Eisenstein thus enacts within his movie the transcendence of the traditional theatrical premise that all conflicts ultimately resolve into two individuals confronting each other or one individual struggling with an internal conflict. The first third of the movie is in a sense a standard Hollywood plot, but it is followed by a very non-Hollywood extension that undermines the premises of the Hollywood plot—that individual character is the basis of good and evil, and that morality is ultimately a mental state found in the minds of the best people. In this movie, good and evil are presented as crowd effects, the results of social structures, and the very notion of individual character is presented as an illusion that must be overcome to achieve a good end.

Eisenstein's film challenges what has become a commonplace of ideological analysis since Althusser: the notion that ideology works by the "creation of subjects." Film theorists such as Peter Wollen and Laura Mulvey follow out the logic of the ideological construction of subjects to conclude that the only filmic way to challenge Hollywood's ideological effects is to produce movies that are essentially devoid of character, not structured as plots, and thus experienced as "unpleasure."[12] For them, discarding the individual would destroy the movie experience, while for Eisenstein, it brings forth a crucial part of the movie experience, by making visible the crowd or the mass, an element of movie structure that film theorists ignore. Eisenstein's films demonstrate that there is—and has been throughout most of film history—an alternative to Hollywood structure that does not simply disrupt and reject the involvement of the audience. Indeed, Eisenstein's films are built very much on bringing the audience to an intense state of involvement, as an audience, a crowd, not as isolated "subjects" or spectators.

Eisenstein seeks to construct intense emotional experiences that are not seen as residing inside individual bodies or directed at individual characters. To do so, Eisenstein has to counter two central elements of "normal" film experience (normal to us because they are fundamental to Hollywood films): the gaze and the structure of gender. The gaze of the camera in Hollywood films functions to define gender differences, and to divide up all collectives into private pairs. Eisenstein, in contrast, uses the gaze of the camera and the structures of gender to unite private individuals into large social bodies.

We can see this process in the Odessa Steps sequence in *Potemkin*. The sequence seems first to borrow traditional gender roles in showing women being attacked by the palace guards: the women appear defenseless, as women stereotypically are, and the guards purely aggressive and violent, stereotypically male. There are elements, however, in the scenes of attack which complicate these stereotypes. For one thing, it is women who stand up to the guards, stopping the general flow of people down the steps and away from the guards. An elderly woman stands and suggests trying to talk to the guards, leading a small group of people up the steps; another woman whose child is shot carries the body towards the guards, saying, "Let me pass, my child is ill." The woman with the dead child is shot and falls in a Christ-like position. The elderly woman doesn't seem to reappear until the very end of this episode, when a Cossack swings a sword and then a woman who looks very much like that elderly woman is shown with blood pouring out through her broken glasses. This final episode is very oddly cut together: we see multiple swings of the sword but they are clearly a single shot repeated multiple times, so that a single act becomes excessively vicious rather than seeming a part of a sequence of strokes. The woman's wound, though, is clearly not made by that swinging sword: she has a puncture wound, not a gash. This small sequence thus does not define any kind of shot/reverse shot of the woman and the Cossack; unlike a Hollywood confrontation, it does not join the two together in a one-to-one relationship. Rather it summarizes all that we have seen before, to provide a powerful emotional climax of the forces in the episode. What is placed together in this moment is the conflict between the two shots, one highlighting a male with a sword, and one a female with glasses that have been punctured. The gender of the characters seems to be repeated by the sword and glasses, and it is unclear how to interpret this repetition. Does the sequence suggest a perverse form of sexuality? Or does the mismatch of the movement of the sword and the wound suggest that the two individuals we are seeing have not interacted at all, but rather the sequence represents the interaction of two groups: males/soldiers attacking females/anonymous people?

The notion that the glasses and the sword label the two individuals as parts of two different groups is supported by the design of the overall scene: lines and circles define the conflicts between male and female throughout this episode. The women who oppose the guards are seen in close-up, often with their mouths open, often with glasses: round faces, round mouths, round glasses, curved shoulders and hips. The guards are all lines: guns with bayonets held rigidly at an angle or all pointed together; legs marching down stairs together, sharply jointed at the knees so they seem stick-figures. Behind both the men and the women, the lines of the stairs themselves define a backdrop that conflicts with both: the guards create a series of lines crossing the lines of the stairs; the women create circles over the lines of stairs. The baby carriage is mostly seen as its large wheels, circles moving across the steps. The final two shots, of the Cossack's swiping sword and the woman's face, summarize these opposed shapes: the sword is a line moving across the screen, like the lines of the marching guards; the face in horror with a wound in the center is all circles and curves and unmoving. Through the associations set up in this sequence, gender become abstracted from individual bodies, in a way that almost never happens in Hollywood movies. Instead of wondering which individual woman and which individual man are paired (say in a man defending some woman he loves or some guard facing the crisis of having to attack a woman he has known in everyday life), the structure of the scene makes us gradually feel that gender has divided groups so completely that there are no interpersonal relations here at all, no individuals looking at each other, no gaze and reverse gaze, just "genders" facing each other abstractly.

A Hollywood film would take this occasion of women being slaughtered as a motive for the good men—led of course by some powerful hero—to become ultraviolent, to wipe out the guards. But the plot after this episode moves in a very different direction. The sense of a large power able to counter the guards does appear, but not as a hero or a contrary group of men, but rather in the form of the ship, which is seen immediately after the Cossack and the woman with broken glasses. The shot of the ship is very odd: it is taken from straight on, with a wide-angle lense, creating a triangle whose base is defined by two cannon which seem to point out to the sides due to the fish-eye effect of the lens; the top of the triangle is the superstructure of the ship. The ship appears large, mountainous, but what dominates the shot are the strangely elegant curves of the decks. This is not a rigid, disciplined source of power like the guards and Cossacks, but rather something organic, related in its curves to the women in the previous sequence. The two prominent guns are ominously pointed directly at the camera, but because of the lens they seem to point out to the sides, and the circles on the ends of the guns are emphasized. In the center of the ship's super-structure is a lifesaving ring, so that the triangular structure of the shot is marked by three similar-sized circles: two gun barrels and a lifesaving ring. The ship comes to save the lives of the people, so I do not think it is accidental that gun barrels are equated in this shot to lifesaving. Further, there is a peculiar sense of the ship as a single human body looking at us, so that the circular guns swelling out to the sides give an effect of breasts—or eyeglasses (fig. 12).

In other words, what comes to save these women is a kind of super-female which is created out of machinery and a large number of men. The ship's guns that will counter the guns of the guards do not carry with them the same connotations of extreme masculinity because the ship's guns are most prominently circles, not lines.

The ship fires on the steps and what we see then are various stones and walls and statues blowing up—never any guards being killed. The emphasis on architectural destruction suggests that the ship is not against the people (not even against the guards), but against the architecture of the state, against the palace. The movie goes to great lengths, in fact, to deny that the revolution is a conflict between humans; it is rather a conflict of institutions. Thus, when the guards face the women, the guards have been transformed into repeated straight lines, which, besides suggesting masculinity, also suggest utter uniformity and unnaturalness; the guards are not humans attacking humans, but pistons and rods being pumped by the machine of the state. The women resisting the guards are not individuals, either, but simply "humanity" as curved flesh and

Fig. 12. The feminine curves of the *Potemkin*.

questioning eyes. When the humans caught up in those institutions end up killing each other, it is tragic because humans don't have to do that: if the institutions could be altered, the humans could join together.

That is of course what ends the movie, in its most non-Hollywood sequence. The movie follows the ship as it goes out to sea, until it faces a convoy of the czar's ships. The confrontation is defined through shots and reverse shots, but not of individuals: we see the *Potemkin*, and then the other ships, back and forth. The shots are long shots, and the men on the *Potemkin* in particular never appear in perfect disciplined order: rather they are massed on various decks, in chaotic crowds, with the strange curved shapes of the decks shaping them not into militaristic lines but into a sense of an organic social body. The entire episode ends up repeating the act that the elderly woman performed in the Odessa Steps sequence: asking those employed by the government to "Join Us." As these words are signaled by flags, we see quick shots and reverse shots from ship to ship; never from individual face to individual face. The camera finally focuses on the *Potemkin*'s guns, which swing straight toward the lens. This swinging motion makes the lines that define the size of the guns shrink and almost disappear as the circles at the ends of the barrels become prominent. One barrel then raises and the camera angle subtly raises with it, until we have dead center in the screen a perfect circle and nothing else. This creates a fearful effect in the audience, as we await a shot coming out of that circle right toward us. But it also fills the screen with the shape from the Odessa Steps episode that was associated with women and with the desire to unite and be family rather than to kill and divide. And just when the gun becomes this perfect circle, word flashes back that the czar's ships will join the *Potemkin*. The confrontation does not end in battle but in union; the men on the czar's ships have reversed the direction their ships are going, so they now accompany the *Potemkin*. Humans have transformed their institutions, making opposed institutions into joined ones. The gun barrel becomes a wedding ring, uniting two collectivities of people in the marriage that is the revolution (figs. 13, 14, and 15).

Eisenstein represents the revolution as the freeing of humans from conflicts created by their institutions.

It might seem that aligning women with unity, peace, and curves is a sexist association, but the entire movie implies that the revolution has to bring men around to assuming some of those female characteristics. The stereotype that aligns men with guns and lines and women with circles and peace is precisely a social institution that has to be altered. The movie further alters the traditional associations of gender by showing men in between their moments of fighting in poses that in Hollywood movies would be associated with voyeuristic views of women's bodies: the men are shown half-naked, sleeping in hammocks. Bill Nichols writes of the "homoerotic languor of Potemkin's sailors in their hammocks."[13] The homoeroticism of these scenes prepares the audience for the final merger of the opposed ships full of men: the revolution will bring men who are set to kill each other to realize that they can love each other instead.

We could say then that the resolution of the movie involves the overcoming of traditional gender roles. Eisenstein converts a gun at its most dangerous to a ring, redefining the gun not as that which repels and expels and keeps at a distance, but as that which unites, an opening, an invitation, a hole through which others can reach and create bonds. Eisenstein suggests that even the human body and the mythic associations with gender characteristics (male organs expel and push out, female organs accept) can be redefined by institutional change, by revolution. Neither the individual nor the gender nor the body itself exists before and outside of vast social structures. It is this sense of radical disruption of the seeming structure of individual human bodies and of the very structures of private life via revolution that is Eisenstein's most radical challenge to Hollywood.

Figs. 13–15. Guns rising . . .

closing in; . . .

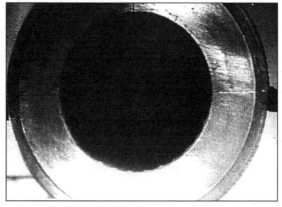

a gun becomes a ring.

Besides modifying gender dichotomies, the movie also modifies the gaze that film theorists have analyzed so well. We can see the movie's modification of the gaze in that final movement of the gun barrel. When the barrel is tilted up, we understand it entirely as an object that shoots and kills, and so as an object that defines a battle over the gaze: who will look and who will be looked at? When the barrel drops to its end-on view and becomes a circle, it becomes ambiguous, and in particular ends up recalling another set of circles besides the ones associated with women and baby carriages: the circles highlighted as glasses at the very beginning of the movie. The first glasses we see are on the officer inspecting meat, and these glasses are clearly identified as distorting and contributing to the lies promulgated by the officers; those glasses are symbols of ideology in operation. At the end of the first battle on the ship, they are seen hanging uselessly on a part of the ship, disconnected from any face. At that point, the movie suggests that their lies have been overcome. They are not shown as broken and destroyed, but only as hanging on the metal ship. I would suggest that this hints at the idea that they can be used again, that the movie is going to move towards a new point of view, a new lens to look through. Glasses proliferate during the Odessa Steps sequence on the faces of numerous persons, men and women, who look back at the guards. Repeatedly such glasses are destroyed, with bullets and swords crashing through them. But then the circles appear again as elements of the ship itself—the guns and the rescue ring hanging above and between the guns. I suggest that the circles of this ship provide an alternative to the glasses that proved so fragile in opposition to guns and swords. And when the gun becomes at the end the circle uniting all the men, it does not represent the disciplining of all the chaos of the sailors hanging off the ship into a rigid unity; rather the "yes" that signals that the enemies will join together sets off celebrations of men loosely lying about all the ships in another scene of "homoerotic exuberance," as Bill Nichols puts it. Nichols contrasts Eisenstein's presentation of a happy crowd with Hollywood's, saying that there is "none of that sterile posing that freezes people into mythic icons, none of that studied iconography of desire that renders actors into stars, none of that condensation of action and agency into the individuated figure of psychological realism that defines bourgeois narratives of fiction and documentary alike."[14]

Eisenstein's vision of the social as something other than a collection of individuals was shared by many early Soviet filmmakers. Another well-known movie, *Man with a Movie Camera*, by Dziga Vertov, uses somewhat different methods to accomplish much the same purpose. The movie has as prologue a manifesto rather like Eisenstein's: Vertov declares that he is going to challenge all the traditional notions of drama, to tell a story without characters, without plot, and without "intertitles" (i.e., without dialogue). The movie has a double structure: it is partly following an entire city during one day, showing people waking, going to work, and then playing in the evening after work. But surrounding the view of a day is another sequence: people watching a movie. This sequence starts with the seats folding down by themselves, people filing in, the projector beginning, and then the movie appearing, the very movie we are watching. The double structure of the movie equates the experience of going to the movies and the experience of going through a work day. Throughout the film, there are moments which also parallel the process of moviemaking and various other processes of daily life (such as opening windows or working in a factory). The movie is, as its title says, about the relationship of man and the movie camera, and what it seems to suggest is that the movie camera is not so much an addition to life as already present in every part of human life: each man has a movie camera, in several senses. Eyes opening are paralleled to shutters on windows opening and to the shutter inside the movie camera: everyone is cutting the world up into shots every day. The assembling of "shots" is then paralleled throughout the movie to various other kinds of work—packaging cigarettes, filling bottles, putting on makeup. The experiences that make up the day in this movie are almost entirely experiences of "construction"—of objects, of people, of movies. The movie becomes a part of an overall process of construction, which produces the entire social system as well as the consciousness of each individual in it.

In creating this vision of the daily construction of reality and self, the movie rather thoroughly undermines the structures which are used to organize and make meaningful a Hollywood movie, in particular the interaction of individuals who learn about each other's characters. The movie gives us no characters, no personalities and no conversations; indeed there is only one body that we see often enough to even begin to recognize, and that is the body of the "man with a movie camera." But he never develops into a personality; rather he is either a voyeur of the experiences everyone else is having or simply part of the overall process of construction, and his body seems as much a part of the passing scene as something he owns.

The movie also includes within it a short sequence that in effect presents in one compact package the elements that make up the essence of Hollywood film narratives: love and death. This short sequence tracks through all the "vicissitudes" that are the central defining structures of standard narratives, whether in Hollywood films, novels, or dramas. In the "love" part of this sequence, we watch very briefly a couple signing a marriage license, then immediately see a very similar scene of a couple signing divorce papers. We only obliquely see the faces of the people signing these papers: what we see mostly are the counter and the papers. Soon after this sequence we see someone else giving birth. In other words, the movie does include those events that traditional narratives say define individual lives—love, marriage, birth, breakup—but it includes them as very small parts of the overarching structure of society, and parts that operate in no distinctive way and with rather less emotional effect than such things as doing one's job or playing in the ocean. The relative emotional weight of love and work in this movie reverses the relative weights in Hollywood films. Further, by having birth appear after the combination of marriage and divorce, the movie disrupts the usual sequence of traditional plots and leaves out what Hollywood would say is the center of that world: love. Marriage, divorce, and birth do not appear events in "private life"; rather they are parts of the overall process of construction of the social order which occurs every day.

The sequence about marriage, divorce, and birth moves directly into a similarly short sequence about violence—an ambulance carries someone who has been injured, the camera focuses in enough to show the bloody body and then cuts abruptly to a funeral procession. We do not see the way the individual who faces violence or death feels, nor do we see the sequence of events that led the person to such bodily suffering, nor the results of that suffering on anyone else. Violence and death seem to be simply events which occur sometimes in every day in a city, and there are mechanisms for structuring those events—ways to move injured or dead bodies so as to maintain the general flow of social construction.

By putting the main emotional elements of traditional drama and Hollywood films into two short, rather unemotional sequences, and surrounding those sequences with much longer and much more affecting sequences about work, movement, play, and the methods of making and projecting movies, the movie recasts the emotional core of life. Life does not, this film says, consist of the movements toward marriage, birth, and death; rather, it consists of the rhythms of work and play. The "vicissitudes" of traditional narrative are not even beginnings and endings of anything much; they are just random events that mix into the overall flow of each day in the city. There is of course a certain irrefutable logic to what this movie presents, strange as it is: most of us spend much more of our time doing our jobs and engaging in play than we do pursuing love or facing violence and death. Indeed, this movie suggests that Hollywood films distort people's senses of what matters so that they overlook how much of their life is controlled and shaped by vast structures and how little is devoted to such things as love and death. Vertov spoke of trying to change the image of the average person "from a dawdling citizen via the poetry of a machine to a perfect electric man. A new man, freed from weight and clumsiness, with the exact and light movements of a machine."[15]

The Man with a Movie Camera is a movie about two machines having a relationship to each other, the man and the movie camera. Vertov seeks to present both of these mechanisms in terms of the motions they perform over and over again, not in terms of any set of desires or emotions which supposedly highlight certain acts (such as marriage) as giving meaning to everything else. As another theorist of the era, Vladimir Voloshnikov, summarizes this view, "The individual consciousness not only cannot be used to explain anything, but, on the contrary, is itself in need of explanation from the vantage point of the social, ideological medium."[16]

This movie also provides an alternative to some commonplace methods of recent critical theory and cultural studies. The movie's claim to be a documentary, a version of history, certainly does not lead it to adopt the "pregeneric plot structures," which Hayden White says are "conventionally used in our culture to endow unfamiliar events and situations with meanings."[17] Nor does the film create "reality effects" or focus on those elements of texts and movies usually studied by cultural critics, which Stuart Hall summarizes as "culture, ideology, language, the symbolic."[18] Vertov's movie implies that focusing on such elements, even if one's goal is to analyze how they are illusions, leads to ignoring the overarching structure of society, which are not much related to "representations" or "the symbolic." Rather remarkably, the movie even implies that ideology—the process which creates "subjects" and "meaningful discourses"—actually functions in only a small part of the social structure.

Such a view may of course be taken as an "old Marxist" view, before the New Left discovered the textuality of everything, but there seems something more: the movie implies that focusing on psychology and love and death and family, as in New Left analyses of ideology, maintains the basic way that capitalist ideology works, maintaining the overemphasis on the individual and the familial and leaving untouched all the time and structure devoted to work and play. In other words, the movie says, we do not have to deconstruct ideology in order to escape it; we can look past it to see how completely everything else is structured—where we walk, what we do when we wake up, how we get dressed, and the ways we view socially produced images in such institutions as the movies. Vertov follows Marx's view that ideology is simply an illusion: "The phantoms formed in the human brain are also, necessarily, sublimates of their material life process, which is empirically verifiable and bound to material premises. Morality, religion, metaphysics, all the rest of ideology and their corresponding forms of consciousness, thus no longer retain the semblance of independence."[19] Movies are usually treated entirely as ideological processes; to consider that a film might function to ignore ideology is a very strange notion.

The usual way to deal with films that have no narrative, no character, and little about love or death is to classify them as avant-garde or experimental, and that is certainly how Vertov's movie has been treated. Political and aesthetic critics alike characterize *Man with a Movie Camera* as essentially an act of disruption, and what is being disrupted is the capitalist West. I have partly joined this way by emphasizing how the movie counters Hollywood structures. However, Vertov and Eisenstein did not conceive of their own films as struggling to disrupt a social order in which they were entrapped; rather they made their films to support what they viewed as the mainstream elements in their country, the early Soviet Union. These movies were not intended to be countercultural performances, but rather to create unity and support for the state. The relatively minor role played by "morality, religion, metaphysics, all the rest of ideology and their corresponding forms of consciousness" in these movies may be a result of the filmmakers' belief that ideology and metaphysical conceptions are no longer operating in the postrevolutionary Soviet Union.

Film theory seems to imply that it is simply not possible to escape ideology: all one can do to counter the effects of ideology is try to create self-deconstructing works that counter themselves. It may very well be that Eisenstein's and Vertov's movies cannot do what they are representing themselves as doing, but it certainly seems that Eisenstein and Vertov *believed* that they could construct movies free of ideology, free of "unconscious" forces that will shape the thoughts and the reactions of their audiences. Their beliefs stand in direct opposition to what I have been trying to show have been the beliefs of Hollywood filmmakers, who have endlessly struggled with "ideological" effects not easily controlled or ignored. I would suggest then that "film theory" is in many ways congruent with the beliefs which underlie Hollywood films, and that such theory is rather unrelated to the conscious efforts of some noncapitalist filmmakers to create movies that are not capitalist.

Vertov and Eisenstein thus present a conundrum for recent theorists: these filmmakers seem to be trying to support a state and its hegemonic discourse without creating ideological effects. Film and cultural studies theories say that is impossible. We could preserve the tenets of recent "theory" by saying that Eisenstein and Vertov are not really trying to support a government, but rather a revolution. Such art may seem to support a government, but only during a period when that government itself is seeking revolution and rapid change. In other words, this anomalous art is just as challenging to *any* social order as film theory suggests anti-Hollywood filmmaking must be, and only appears to support a government during a period when the government itself seems to be challenging the social order as well. Once that government settles down, there will again be subjects, reality effects, narratives, and everything upon which cultural studies methods focus. This is a thoroughly plausible idea, and Eisenstein's later works under Stalin do seem to restore subjects and reality and classical narrative structures. But then we have this disturbing thought that the methods of cultural studies analysis are applicable only during periods of settled cultural order. Perhaps they do not function during periods of revolution, when art forms actually change. Does this suggest that cultural studies analyses, even though they may talk of resistance and the deconstruction of hegemonic forms, are somewhat conservative in the sense that they are not relevant to the possibility of a revolution, but only to changes within a relatively stable ideological system? If that is so, then film theorists are fundamentally in agreement with Hollywood filmmakers and not in agreement with Vertov and Eisenstein.

I suspect that film theorists would not be very disturbed by the notion that Eisenstein and Vertov provide better ways to counter capitalist ideology than what critical theories advocate. Eisenstein and Vertov clearly share the Marxist tradition that led up to the recent critical methods. The political alternative to Hollywood would still be found on the Left. Much more disturbing to the tenets of film theory—and to cultural studies in general—are some early Nazi films, which show that breaking free of Hollywood forms might lead to fascism. Leni Riefenstahl performs a "discarding" of the individual nearly as complete as Eisenstein's, but with a very different political conclusion. Russell Berman describes fascist art as marking a "transition from a bourgeois age of subjective interiority, the site of a literary culture, to a postindividualism of visible power."[20] In looking beyond the subject, Riefenstahl does not find the swirling energetic masses of Eisenstein and Vertov, but rather the highly disciplined and monumental formations of marching bodies which unify into a single social "body," which somehow is identical to the body of a dictator. Siegfried Kracauer describes the process as one that turns "an amorphous body of anonymous, fragmented particles"—all the separate individuals—into a "mass ornament" which then undergoes a "monumental mating" with the "heroic body" of the leader, creating a "megamyth."[21] This process, as we will see in Riefenstahl's films, is as clearly based on a rejection of capitalist ideology as Eisenstein's and Vertov's films.

It might seem, however, that the ultimate focus on a dictator, a single leader, suggests that fascist theory restores a strange form of "individualism." And the title of Riefenstahl's most famous film, *Triumph of the Will*, seems to point to an internal quality of the individual psyche, will, as the focus of the movie. The notion of will or even "personality" does have an important role in fascist theory, and Hitler writes in *Mein Kampf* about this quality as crucial in distinguishing fascism from communism:

> The folkish philosophy is basically distinguished from the Marxist philosophy by the fact that it not only recognizes the value of race, but with it the importance of personality, which it therefore makes one of the pillars of its entire edifice.[22]

Hitler may sound as much an individualist as John Stuart Mill in advocating a state based on personality, but fascist "personality" has nothing to do with focusing on the "personal" interests of each one in society, and certainly nothing to do with having society run to support various individuals' self-interests. Quite the contrary: Hitler identifies the ideal folkish personality with "the self-sacrificing will to give one's personal labor and if necessary one's own life for others."[23] He argues that it is this quality that marks the greatness of the Aryan race: "The Aryan is not greatest in his mental qualities as such, but in the extent of his willingness to put all his abilities in the service of the community."[24] In contrast to this Aryan self-sacrificing "personality," Hitler describes the worst influence on the state as self-interest, which he labels a Jewish trait: "In the Jewish people the will to self-sacrifice does not go beyond the individual's naked instinct of self-preservation."[25] Having no ability to devote themselves to the community, "The Jews possess no culture-creating force of any sort."[26]

We might then distinguish Hitler's notion of personality from the liberal notions which underlie Hollywood filmmaking by saying that Hitler wants a "cultural personality," a personality that perhaps paradoxically becomes most evident when the individual loses or "sacrifices" all idiosyncratic qualities and becomes instead the embodiment of what is deeply common to the entire community. The ideal personality then is one that is completely identical to the community, and in effect there can be only one such personality. In some ways this gets represented as the identical appearance of long rows of persons who gather in geometric arrangements and appear to act and think identically, but it is most completely represented by the one body which is declared identical to the state in the repeated cheer, "Hitler is Germany! Germany is Hitler!" Hitler argues that the culmination of personality is the elimination of democracy: "the folkish state must free all leadership and especially the highest—that is, the political leadership—entirely from the parliamentary principle of majority rule . . . and instead absolutely guarantee the right of personality . . . the decision will be made by one man."[27]

If we examine the movies of Leni Riefenstahl and a few other Nazi filmmakers, we can gain an understanding of how this concept of "personality" is quite unlike that found in Hollywood films. For one thing, the "best" person in Hollywood movies is usually the one we get to know the best: the audience develops a "personal" relationship with the hero; we watch the leader talk with his buddies, we understand his feelings, we identify with his emotions. Further, we see stars in multiple movies taking different roles, so we separate the "person" from the role, in a kind of transcendence of idiosyncratic qualities and "personality traits" over particular acts or decisions or relationships to communities. The Hollywood star can enter any community and become a central figure in it. Hitler is represented as emerging from and being the center of exactly one community, the Aryan nation. Hollywood stars bridge the private and the public; Hitler submerges the private, redefining personality as an entirely public phenomenon. Hence we never see Hitler talking to one or two people in Riefenstahl's documentary, and we do not learn about his humor or his pleasantness; indeed his "private life" seems utterly irrelevant to his role as "personality" in the folkish state. Hitler is a monumental "star" of a rather different kind than Hollywood creates.

And Hitler is not the only person to acquire this peculiar "public" personality which replaces private idiosyncrasy. The documentary *Olympia* traces a similar process occurring in the construction of athletes' "personalities." In that movie we do get to see athletes in their off-stage moments: warming up, acting rather funny, relaxing between events. But when they enter their performances as athletes, they shed these off-stage personas and become statuesque. In Riefenstahl's recording of athletic performances, bodies lose their oddities and become instead "beautiful."

A way to understand the nature of beautiful bodies in *Olympia* is to note that the film is divided into two halves, "The Festival of Beauty" and "The Festival of the People." The distinction between the two halves is not a distinction between private life, where beauty functions as it does in Hollywood love stories, and public life, where the people reign. Rather, beauty is the physical embodiment of the "people"; beauty is created by individuals suppressing their private oddities, "sacrificing" their selves in the name of athletic perfection. Beauty is that which makes a single body serve as the focus for a wave of emotion in the crowd: the athlete transforming the human body into a statuesque perfection elicits and reflects the joy of the crowd cheering. In *Olympia*, we watch how ordinary persons become "beautiful" through the disciplinary process of athletic practice, a process that bears considerable similarity to what Vertov shows in *Man with a Movie Camera*: the repetition of certain motions constructs the essence and value of a person far more than any "psychological" quality.

In *Triumph of the Will*, the creation of beauty is somewhat more mysterious. Hitler is the very definition of "beauty" in that movie even though his body is not in any obvious sense "beautiful." Hitler transcends not only whatever private, idiosyncratic character traits he might have, but even the distinctive features of his physical body and the peculiar gestures and rhythms of his speech. *Triumph of the Will* shows the "culture-creating" personality emerging in some mysterious way without actually being visible: what Hitler calls "personality" can only be shown in the repeated flips back and forth between the leader and the crowd response. The entire movie is structured to balance the crowd against the images of Hitler's body, and to lead us in the audience to that perspective from which we are seeing or trying to see (since it remains invisible) the "culture-creating personality," not the individual characters and bodies we are familiar with from everyday life. The Nuremberg rally creates from the collection of bodies of individual people this larger, transcendent perspective, and then places as the core of our experience of transcendence the body of Hitler.

We can trace the way that Riefenstahl places Hitler's body in this transcendent position. The opening images are of clouds seen through plane windows, presented via a camera that pans part way around, almost turning back inside the plane, then cutting to other clouds. The series of shots never has a reverse shot to show us the plane or the person who is looking at the clouds, and we become eager to find the person who can provide such a heavenly perspective. Eventually, the camera descends through the clouds to buildings, seen from above, and finally we have a reverse shot of the plane: this then seems to be the view of the buildings, of the structure on the ground, looking at the structure in the sky, and still there is no single body through whose eyes we might be looking. The first people we see are dots on the ground, which soon coalesce into very sharp lines, particularly in one shot of marchers turning a right angle, viewed from almost directly above. The movement from clouds to buildings to people suggests metaphoric interpretations: descent from heaven; gradual construction of Germany from "nothing" (white clouds) to architectural arrangements (buildings, streets), inserting people as a collective, architectural feature. When we finally see individual faces, they are presented as details of the lines of people who have been marching, now stationary, but with their hands outstretched in salutes, so that the faces appear as part of a vast array of diagonal lines. Individual faces blur together as we pass by them, becoming part of the sequence of repeated shapes. The titles preceding these shots describe Germany as having undergone a "passion" and a "rebirth," so the opening sequence traces the descent from heaven of a reborn nation and a reborn God: an incarnation mimicking Christ's passion and resurrection. When Hitler finally reveals himself, the camera keeps sliding off of him to the crowd cheering, implying that he is not separate or self-contained: the worshiping crowds are the defining quality of his body. Hitler is godlike because he creates worshiping crowds, not because of some quality in his body itself. We follow his body for about as long as we first remained in the heavenly perspective, so that the body of Hitler gains the "volume" of screen time and space to fill the heavenly perspective.

The opening sequences could be considered an unusual version of what suture theory ends up speculating about: the opening in the sky sets up a very strong sense of the "Absent one," the implied controller of what we are allowed to see.[28] According to suture theory, the sense of an "absent one" creates anxiety because the absent one seems to have much more power than "we" do as we watch. In Hollywood practice, according to suture theory, a reverse shot relieves this anxiety by revealing that there is no controlling cameraman. The world is "sutured" by this reverse shot, stitched together into a seamless whole controlled by no one and thereby giving us a sense that "we" are the privileged ones allowed to see everything. Riefenstahl's opening sequences take a different tack. When we see Hitler, we get a whole series of shot/reverse shot pairs, always from his one set of eyes to the thousands of eyes of the crowd. Unlike the sequences in Hollywood movies, Riefenstahl's sequences do not stitch the world together in the two reversed points of view: rather the two remain unequal and seemingly different in kind. One is the single, unified gaze of Hitler; the other the multiple gazes of the crowd. We are too strongly identified with the crowd to have any doubt which of these two kinds of gazes we share. We are drawn to Hitler's eyes, wishing we could look through them, but the only way to do so is to join the crowd and look at him.

Hitler's eyes then represent a kind of gaze that we can only dream about. He occupies the position of the "Absent One" and thereby "has all the attributes of the mythically potent symbolic father: potency, knowledge, transcendental vision, self-sufficiency, and discursive power."[29] The opening from the sky sets up the perspective of "transcendental vision" and vast knowledge, and Hitler's head and arm create a sense of potency and self-sufficiency: he can stand alone against and equal to all the crowds of people he passes.

Riefenstahl's opening sequence does not then operate according to the mechanisms specified by suture theory: the anxiety created by the sense of our vision being controlled by some Absent One is converted into a desire to be controlled by a godlike person. Instead of being released into a "reality" in which everyone is roughly free to have their own perspective in a reality "sutured" together and so be free of the Absent One who seemed to control us, we are drawn into a desire for the joy of worshiping just such a controlling personality. In his final speech, there is even an odd sense that he is surprised by the powerful response his words are producing—his control over the crowd is beyond his own individual understanding. He is not a person in the sense that a character in a Hollywood movie is a person, and his "personality" is not inside him, but rather is a monumental construct of his relation to the crowd. Viewing this face does not take us into his head as faces do in Hollywood films; rather viewing this face puts us into the crowd, and gives us the "pleasure" of having our vision given to us, the pleasure of being controlled, by this person whose body is the marker of a superhuman perspective that transcends even the mind inside that body.

Triumph of the Will orchestrates the experience of becoming part of a far greater "body" than any individual body and aims to convey that experience as crucial: it aims at conveying what Hitler describes in *Mein Kampf* as crucial to the formation of the mass emotions that support his regime:

> The man who is exposed to grave tribulations, as the first advocate of a new doctrine, absolutely needs that strengthening which lies in the conviction of being a member and a fighter in a great comprehensive body. And he obtains an impression of this body for the first time in the mass demonstration. When . . . he steps for the first time into a mass meeting and has thousands and thousands of people of the same opinions around him, when, as a seeker, he is swept away by three or four thousand others into the mighty effect of suggestive intoxication and enthusiasm, when the visible success and agreement of thousands confirm to him the rightness of the new doctrine . . . then he himself has succumbed to the magic influence of what we designate as "mass suggestion." The will, the longing, and also the power of thousands are accumulated in every individual. The man who enters such a meeting doubting and wavering leaves it inwardly reinforced: he has become a link in the community.[30]

The concept of a "great comprehensive body" is crucially connected to the notion of "personality" as Hitler defines it: there is an organic wholeness to the masses when they come together in the fascist regime that makes them "one body" with one personality, a complete reflection of the one leader. Riefenstahl throughout her filmmaking career focused on the body, but never as an indicator of individual differences; rather as that which can be a representation of the whole.

I suggest that Riefenstahl was exploring a rather different answer to the same question Griffith was exploring, as we saw in Chapter 2: how to deal with the demise of the royal body in the individualist state. Fascist theory restores such a body, but without the peculiar ways that family defined it in the monarchy: Hitler is the body that can accept all desires but not because his family is identified with the state, but rather because his mind and soul, his "personality," is identified with the crowd reaction. Hitler's body is not defined by being gazed at by a lover—as were the idealized leaders in Griffith's movies—but rather by exchanging gazes with a crowd and with the transcendent Reich embodied in symbols. The rebirth of Germany, which is the subject of *Triumph of the Will*, is the rebirth of the imperial center, reborn not through transcendent sexuality that generates kingship, but through a transcendent vision that relies on public desires expressed between the leader and the crowd. This transcendent vision is itself made visible by public performances of crowds and leaders, which create something that is supposed to replace individual identity. One of the most influential fascist writers, Ernst Junger, theorized the process of creating such replacements of identity, calling for an "overriding Gestalt of authority" that could "organize the masses and abolish private identity."[31] Fascism claims that the multiplicity of identities of citizens is an illusion created by the fragmentation of modern society, an illusion to be overcome by fascism.

Olympia traces a similar sense of modern Germany as a rebirth of an ancient monumental body that was once scattered, broken apart. The film begins with opening shots of clouds as well, then moves to ruins scattered over fields, to pillars, and then to the whole Acropolis: from the formlessness of clouds to a destroyed structure to a relatively complete structure, as if the architecture of Greece were reassembling itself. As in *Triumph of the Will*, the structures of architecture allow the emergence of ideal bodies. From the Acropolis, we cut to a single pillar, which the camera pans down, and a statue's face emerges behind it, tilted sideways with an arm going straight up and bending to the head, so that we have a sense of human form continuing the architecture. Then we get a series of dissolves of statue faces, which are animated to move across each other. This opening is in effect showing the effort to assemble body parts that have been separated. But what is assembled is not one distinctive body, as it would be in a Hollywood movie; body parts here are not presented as "part" of a single whole individual, but are rather assembled with other similar body parts. Faces dissolve into other faces, and later, hands into hands, and in the events of the athletic competition that we later watch, one straining arm into another, one churning leg into another, so that we see each "individual" athlete as part of an athletic event created by multiple bodies. The individual striving for athletic perfection becomes impersonal, joining others also striving for such perfection, who all become pure forms, each separate peculiar human transformed into a common ideal formal structure.

The statues crossing each other climax in two faces, one in profile, one full front, with the profile slowly moving across the other until it almost merges, the edge of the profile fitting into the shape of shadows across the full front, almost creating a Picassoesque dual face, half-profile, half-frontal. This strangely mixed face dissolves into a statue of a discus thrower, which appears to rotate and then dissolves into a living discus thrower. This transition from a statue made to seem as if it were moving to a human actually moving implies, as *Triumph of the Will* did, that Riefenstahl is tracing the emergence of the human body as the extension and development of rigid, unmoving stone, not as the contradiction of stone. As the fascist theorist Junger puts it, the new body created by the new regime is "more metallic, its surface is galvanized, the bone structure is evident, and the traits are clear and tense. The gaze is steady and fixed . . . a new landscape where one is represented neither as a person nor as an individual but as a type."[32]

This transition from fragments to a structural whole also suggests the very form of film itself—the creation of motion from the assembling and precise structuring of a series of still shots. As human bodily motion "evolves" from the artificial animation of images of statues, we gain a sense of human motion as a series of still positions, a series of poses. Athletics is perhaps a kind of reversal of the action of film: the shaping of fluid bodily motions into a series of "stills," so that the body at every moment is a photograph of an ideal form. Athletics is the shaping of reality, of fluid Euclidean space, until it is for a time geometrically perfect. Hollywood films usually seek to find within the rigid structures of society small spaces where individuals can fluidly express their idiosyncratic and relatively ungeometric personalities. Riefenstahl seeks to eliminate those moments of unstructured fluidity and thereby convert the private "personality" in all its idiosyncrasy into the public structure, into the type.

A crucial part of the construction of the human body in *Olympia* is the creation of a peculiar and non-Hollywood sense of gender. First the movie continues through a series of parallel shots of male bodies: throwing a discus, throwing a shot, throwing a javelin. Then a shotput is thrown and seems to be caught, and we move to a montage of hands waving back and forth—all male bodies. Then there is a similar array of female bodies, but they are using hoops, which are large circles that they wave about rather than propelling away from themselves. Then three nude female bodies perform what appears to be a ritual that appears more dance than athletics: seated in a triangle, they press their palms together, forming a circle of human bodies, hands waving apart then pressing together. It might seem odd to have sexualized, naked dance numbers in Nazi films, but actually they were quite common. Herbert Marcuse notes that Nazi Germany instigated a "new cult of nudity in art and entertainment," which combined with repressive social policies about sexuality in private life to "connect released sexual desire to an external state end."[33] Nazi musicals often feature female dance troupes but, Terri Gordon notes, unlike American musicals, "the deeper meaning of the [Nazi musicals] lies not in the romantic life of the girls but, rather, in the communal ethos that binds them together."[34]

The communal ethos in Riefenstahl's sequence is represented by the merging of the three women into one body with six arms, a Hindu goddess. Then a flame appears at the bottom of the screen, from the off-stage loins of the goddess (figs. 16, 17, and 18).

This flame eventually takes over the screen, and from it there appears a man holding a torch. The rest of the opening of *Olympia* traces the running of the torch from Greece to Germany to finally light the cauldron of flame that opens the Olympic Games. The opening thus presents the flame of the ancient Olympic spirit as something first "lit" by a collective female body which is represented in terms of circular, fluid motions, from which emerges a man in phallic rigidity topped by the fluid flickering flame. The small light which males carry from Greece to Germany in this movie derives from a much larger female flame which is the origin of the Olympic spirit. We might read a reference to Riefenstahl's own role as a female filmmaker in this image of light provided by females and in the sense that from that female light is created the sculpted fascist man.

There is another moment that also provides a sense of the origin of the flame, but this time from a light spread out across the ocean. This moment occurs as the runner takes off. First there is a cut to a shot of the ocean with a line of light on it stretching from the horizon, from a sun or moon just out of sight, to the shore. A runner with the torch appears at the edge of this shot as the scene gradually dissolves to a scene of him running along a different shore. The line of light remains until he just about reaches the bottom of it on the screen, at which point the dissolve is completed, so his torch replaces the line of light from the heavenly body across water. Then there is a triple superimposition: the runner along the shore, now at the top of the screen; the line of light across the water, now stretching out below his torch; and over both of these, images of waves breaking. The light seems then to be breaking through the waves, creating formal order out of the natural chaos and the natural power of the moving water. I would suggest that the shot creates a sense that the light that organizes human striving (athletics, politics) comes from the oceanic divine, and the oceanic is symbolically associated with the mother. We might even see a hint of early film technology in this shot: to allow the fire to be projected without burning everything up, we need to shine the light through water, as the water lens allowed the

Figs. 16–18. Dancing female bodies . . .

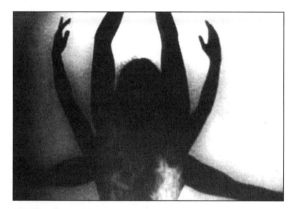

merging . . .

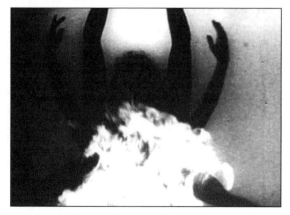

to give birth to the Olympic flame.

early projectors to work without burning up the film. Riefenstahl's movie thus opens with the necessity of merging the fluid and circular with the linear and statuesque, the female with the male, to create the spirit of athletic ideals. The fluid and circular does not constitute an image of an "individual" or a private woman but rather represents a collective source identified with divine goddesses.

The end of the film returns to this imagery of light connecting heaven and earth, and reverses the sequence from feminine circularity to male linearity. In the last sequence, shots of male divers are cut together, so that we see one after another a series of divers leaping off the same diving board into space. The camera is placed to the side and below these bodies, so that the divers seem to be moving up and sideways, never down, as if they are leaping up to fly into the clouds. Finally one diver remains suspended horizontally across the clouds as light increases behind him, becoming so bright that his body turns into a black silhouette, then fades out. The divers, each striving to more perfectly become an idealized form, together achieve flight, ascension back to the clouds from which the spirit and light and flame of the Olympics descended. The divers repeating the same motions in effect become one body ascending, as the runners at the beginning of the movie replacing each other become one runner going farther than any single body could go: each becomes a "link in the community," part of the "great comprehensive body" that is the Olympics.

The continuation of the movie after the diving sequence reverses the progression of the opening sequence: this time the linear motion which was created by males turns into a circular many-armed figure, reminiscent of the opening female goddesses. This final progression is presented as an overview of the whole stadium, taken entirely in long shots. First the camera starts looking out at the clouds (the realm into which the divers disappeared), and then descends to the stadium, from which rows of searchlights turn on, creating a pillared structure like the Acropolis, made of projected light: the Greek structure recreated by modern technology, by the very technology that allows filmmaking. The pillars of light bend together and the camera moves up them so we expect something to be illuminated by them all, a center revealed. But instead of reaching that center in the sky, most of the pillars of light dissolve and we see through the space they occupied the cauldron of flame with smoke all around it: the vertical individual lines of light, like erect humans, dissolve into the fluid and flickering collective flame which was the original divine source of the Olympic spirit.

The cauldron dissolves into an image of a row of pikes with flags on them bending to have wreaths placed around them, a merger of linear/phallic and circular/feminine. Then the pillars of light reappear through the smoke and once again bend together, but this time we move up them all the way to a center. There, where we would expect to see something illuminated by all these lights, a vision of what belongs in the spotlight, we get a strange reversal: the lights join together creating a brilliant confluence of whiteness that fills almost the entire screen. The lights seem no longer then to be shining into this center, but rather to be radiating from it, like a sun (figs. 19 and 20).

This sun is an impossible result of searchlights shining up from the ground: no matter how many lights are focused on the same spot in the sky, they will not join in a central starlike radiance unless there is something there to reflect them—a screen. What is in effect revealed then by following the lights up is a screen that reflects back on us, creating the illusion that it is the source of light. This final effect makes what we are seeing identical to the structure of projection and screen reflection that occurs in the theater: light is radiating out of the projector lens behind us, which we never look at, but the screen at the front of the theater converts that light into a star that shines on us (even blinding us) and seems to be the light source in the theater. If the screen is only the reflection of the real source of light hidden in the projection room above and behind us, similarly, the light that seems to shine from the Nazi state, from the leader (the light that seemed to radiate from the stage in *Triumph of the Will* as Hitler spoke) is only a reflection of some hidden source, of a projector of light that creates the images that we see as Hitler and as the fascist light. That hidden source is both the sun of a divinity and the filmmaker, who runs projectors to create the images before us. The image of a sun also returns the linear pillars to a circular shape with multiple "arms" radiating from it, recalling the image of the woman with many arms radiating in all directions, a goddess figure, from which the fire emerged that lit the torch of the Olympics. This ending thus returns to the suggestion of the opening sequence that there is a female origin of the light which creates the phallic power of men.

The beautiful male bodies which permeate Riefenstahl's films do not then give phallic origin to the state: rather they gain their beauty and their passion from a fire projected from a female source. The "male gaze," the line of sight that is so powerfully analyzed in spectator theory, in this movie is presented as deriving from a diffuse, flickering, circular female energy that creates the light to be arranged into a gaze. The end

Figs. 19–20. Pillars of light bending together . . .

to magically form a sun.

of the movie returns the male gaze with what is in effect an even more powerful female gaze. The spectator of either gender is involved in a kind of sexual exchange with the camera, drawn into a public ritual of viewing and being viewed. As Terri Gordon describes the effect of this movie's presentation of beautiful bodies, "The image is a seductive one, inviting the viewers to join the cult of the body and take part in the organic wholeness of the social sphere."[35]

To see how Riefenstahl envisions a quite distinctive role for a female in creating the gaze that defines the nation, we can turn to an earlier narrative movie she made, *The Blue Light*. That movie shows a striking rejection of Hollywood clichés about male and female gazes: the attempt of males to take control of the female gaze by installing the female in a love relationship destroys the fire that generates the spirit of the state. In that film, Junta, a mountain girl, has a strange relationship to a cave of crystals high up on a mountain, from which some nights a blue light shines down into the town. She is the only person who can enter that cave, because only she knows the way up the mountain. When the light shines, young men are hypnotically driven to climb toward the crystals, and all fall to their deaths. When we see the light shining from the mountain, it appears very much like a film projector's light, a beam emerging from a hole on the mountain, spreading out to illuminate and draw men to it. The light in effect creates a film in which the men must act out their role of tragic self-sacrifice. The cave full of crystals is another of the images, like the many-armed goddess and the sun at the end of *Olympia*, of multiplicity connected to femaleness, and as in that movie, this female power draws men to leave their private lives and engage in mythic acts of sacrificing themselves to the spirit of the mountain. Susan Sontag describes the mountain as a "high mystic goal which was later to become concrete in Fuhrerworship, . . . which invites the ultimate affirmation of and escape from the self—into the brotherhood of courage and death."[36]

Into this mythos of a tragic fascism, a rather Hollywood plot is introduced: a man from outside the town seduces Junta; they frolic on the hillside and she shows him how to climb to the cave of crystals. But the man does not share in that "high mystic goal" of dying for the Majestic Mountain. He sees in the crystals only a source of destruction, which can be converted into a source of wealth by being mined and sold. He leads the townspeople up the secret path so they can ransack the crystals and become rich. Then an eerie sequence occurs in which Junta falls to her death from the mountain. From that we cut to a modernized version of the town. The young men no longer sacrifice themselves; instead they sell books of the myth and are rich from the money they received for the crystals. This story is thus a tale of the replacement of the mythical city by the city of money. The agent of this transformation is an "outsider," someone not of the "race" of the town, and the conversion of the town is in effect the loss of its racial roots, of that which went beyond the material and the physical. The mythical, the light emerging from crystals that transformed consciousness and led the townspeople to that "self-sacrifice," which Hitler called the essence of the Aryan spirit, is reduced to the material—glittery gems. The woman who could project the mythical is reduced to a dead body, a piece of matter.

It is striking that the cause of Junta's reduction from mythical status to mere matter is her falling in love. Before the outsider came, Junta had no relationship to any individuals; nobody in the town was even willing to look at Junta. The townspeople drove her away, especially from the young men. The outsider thus brings into this world what we could call the individualized "male gaze" of Hollywood, the gaze of a lover, and it is this gaze which destroys the mythical, if rather tragic, quality of the town.

The outsider, though presented as quite an elegant fellow, is a prototype of the Jew, who converts culture and its special superhuman relation to a people into a universal object of exchange, into money. As Hitler wrote, the Jew brings self-preservation or self-interest as the prime goal, replacing self-sacrifice. Self-interest makes all interactions exchanges, as each person must gain. There is no sacrificial joining together to create a community, and hence in Hitler's terms no "Aryan spirit." Even the story of Junta becomes an object of exchange, found in a book circulated to everyone who visits the town. The movie does not provide any image of another way to make use of the self-sacrificing spirit created by the light, but *Mein Kampf* does make such a suggestion: the town needs a leader who can organize the self-sacrifice inspired by the magical light and turn the town into a superhuman community full of self-sacrificing people—a fascist totality.

In her last movie, *Tiefland*, Riefenstahl returns to the image of a woman who instills some magical desire in men, but in this movie, it is by her own dancing, not by a light coming from a cave in a mountain: the desire has become sexual. Yet this movie stills remains far from Hollywood tropes, because it suggests what was evident in *The Blue Light*: the desire for the woman as a private possession is what destroys the community. The woman has to be accepted as a public figure, a dancing self, tied only to the surrounding mountains, not to a private house within the town.

105

Riefenstahl's movie turns the question of whether the dancer performs in public or in private into a central element of the plot. The leader of the town takes the dancer and installs her in a private world, shielding her from public view. This act of removing from the public what would "feed" their desires is paralleled to another act of this leader: he takes the water that runs into town from the mountains and uses it to water his bulls, which he breeds for his own glory. The breeding of bulls is precisely an image of using the power of leadership to promote a false sexuality, the same thing he does when he uses his power to keep the dancer in his private house, dancing only for him. The misuse of the woman is equated to the misuse of natural resources: he is creating a false image of male power by removing from the public the sexuality, the "libido," the "blood," the fluid that should "water" the nation and help it breed the superior race.

It is also crucial that the leader does not marry the dancer, and so does not really form a social "body" with her, but rather subordinates her to himself as an individual. Because he needs money, he marries a wealthy woman instead, and arranges for the dancer to marry a shepherd, with the proviso that he will continue his sexual relationship with her because this arranged husband is an idiot. The leader thus tries to make two women serve to increase his individual stature.

However, his plot fails because the shepherd has been in love with the dancer ever since he first saw her dance, and when he realizes what has been arranged, he kills the leader and goes off with the dancer to live in the mountains. It might seem that this ending is an image of restoring private love. But the movie militates against such a reading. When the shepherd kills the leader, the murder mirrors an earlier scene where the shepherd killed a wolf feeding on his sheep. When the shepherd confronts the leader, he says, "Ah, the wolf," before attacking. In other words, he is not fighting for his own private life in fighting the leader; rather he is acting as a good shepherd, as a leader that the town needs. Furthermore, the act of killing the leader is staged as a performance, with the townspeople as an audience that ultimately joins the performance by keeping the leader from escaping, pushing him back into the arms of the shepherd. The townspeople thus become the chorus in the "dance number" of the orchestrated removal of this bad leader. After this number, the return of the shepherd to the mountains is not a return to privacy but to his role as a caretaker of a multitude, with no fixed abode, no private house. In the final shot, the shepherd and dancer do not enter a cottage in the hills; rather they are framed by romantic shots of mist and mountains. The dancer's being taken up into the mountains seems then the restoration of the romantic mythic source of culture, the restoration of water and sheep to feed and clothe the people.

Water plays the role in this film that light does in *The Blue Light* and that flame does in *Olympia*: all three represent conduits for the transference of the divine or the superhuman into the modern state. This infusion of the divine is also represented by the development of the males in all three movies: in *Tiefland*, the shepherd transforms from an unsophisticate at the beginning to a skilled performer when he kills the bad leader; in *Olympia*, the athletes first appear as young people doing rather amusing exercises, then transform into cosmic athletic figures; in *Triumph of the Will*, we early on see boys clowning around who later create lines of beautifully disciplined soldiers. In all three movies, there is a process portrayed whereby beautiful masses of male bodies are produced by the metaphoric infusion of spirit from female goddesses, represented as acting through fire and water and light.

The politics of these movies is muddied by Riefenstahl's uncertain relationship to Nazi ideology. We can see the problem in an issue that has haunted the history of *Tiefland*: Riefenstahl used concentration-camp inmates, Roma, for the townspeople. While the Nazi regime had rounded up these Roma as a type that should be eliminated to restore the pure cultural roots of Germany, Riefenstahl's use of them to represent the people who need a new form of leader could imply that she has a different view of race. She claimed later that her movies were seeking an ideal leader who could be a mythic soul for all of humanity. In *Olympia*, she similarly portrays African and Asian athletes—not merely Aryans—as beautiful. She seems to come close to advocating a universal beauty, not a racial one. However, I suspect that her inability in *Tiefland* to create any image of a new leader who has a real relationship to the peasants suggests that she cannot quite envisage Hitler's becoming the shepherd of these "foreign" sheep. When we follow the dancer and the shepherd into the mountains, we are seeing the racially "pure" unite with the mountains and leave the mongrelized hordes in the city behind. Riefenstahl cannot quite unite the mythic and the modern.

There is a difference between the monumental figures created in these movies and the stars created by Hollywood films. Hollywood celebrity is not mythic status: rather it takes the form of what individualism needs, namely a mass interest in the private character of those turned into celebrities. And celebrities, for all their power in influencing mass reactions and all their seeming superhuman status, do not disrupt the notion that everyone is merely human. The norm of the narrative of celebrity is that it is the private self, the peculiar talent or character or bodily beauty of the star that creates the celebrity status. In Riefenstahl's films, it is a mythic something that leads Junta, the dancer, Hitler, and the athletes beyond their private selves to their public roles. Griffith, as we saw in Chapter 2, was torn between these two visions, the monumental and the individualist: he tried to install the collective inside the private mind, but could not see how there would be enough room for the truly monumental. Hence he proposed supplemental collective bodies such as the KKK or the movies to maintain the monumental.

In the next chapter, we will follow the career of a filmmaker who moved across this divide, shifting in his moviemaking from the attempt to imagine a society devoted to the worship of the monumental to devoting his films to creating a society in which the vast resources of the state are devoted to supporting private individuals.

5

FROM LOVE OF THE STATE TO THE STATE OF LOVE: FRITZ LANG'S MOVE FROM WEIMAR TO HOLLYWOOD

*I*n previous chapters, I showed that in movies from Hollywood and early Soviet and fascist countries, the masses are represented as a seething cauldron of emotions that can yet become an important part of the overall social structure. In Hollywood films, the seething masses mold private loves, while in collectivist movies, they turn into organized mass movements. Fritz Lang, working first in pre–Nazi Germany and then in Hollywood, created movies that can be seen as meditations on both ways of using the crowd. At the center of many of his movies is a riot, when the crowd has intense passions that need to be structured. In Lang's greatest German movies, the structure comes from a leadership that can organize the masses, while in his Hollywood movies, the structure is created out of private relationships. We might say Lang followed the political philosophies in which he found himself, but that would be too simple. His movies' endings often feel false, and in that falseness we see that Lang could adapt to the opposite milieus because he had serious doubts about both systems.

Collective experience in Lang's movies is much too powerful to be tamed into either neatly organized marching bodies or private love affairs. Individuals fail to be satisfactory leaders and they fail to stand apart from the crowd. Tom Gunning summarizes Lang's vision: "Lang is less concerned with the psychological complexity of characters, with their interiority (whose existence I think he doubts), than with their interface with social systems, with technology and politics. . . . For Lang individuality and even desire always become subsumed into larger impersonal

109

and often sinister systems."[1] Gunning does not devote much space to considering Lang's movies in terms of the differing political and social systems of Weimar and Hollywood, instead arguing that throughout his career, Lang presented individual lives as subsumed to what Gunning dubs the "Destiny Machine," a vast system operating without any comprehensible agenda at all, and hence only ambiguously related to any social politics. I agree that Lang's politics are ambiguous, but this ambiguity allowed his movies to deeply reflect (in a cracked mirror we might say) those differing political milieus.

One way to get at the difference between Lang's German and Hollywood films is to start with his own description of the differing audience expectations he faced: "So over there [in Germany] the hero in a motion picture should be a superman. Whereas in a democracy he had to be Joe [sic] Doe."[2] The superhuman in Lang's vision is the person who can control the sinister Destiny Machine; Joe Doe in Hollywood is the image of "everyone" in the crowd; if it were made entirely of Joe Does, it would no longer be threatening.

Lang's Weimar movies trace out two different kinds of superhuman figures: mythic leaders, who struggle to bring nobility and morality to the irrational machinery of the universe, such as the *Nibelungen* heroes or Freder and Maria in *Metropolis*; and manipulators, who remain hidden while using the social machinery for their own sinister ends, such as Dr. Mabuse, Rotwang in *Metropolis*, and, in a strange way, Hans Beckert, the child-murderer in *M*. In many of these movies, as we shall see, Lang suggests parallels between the superhuman manipulation of the social order and moviemaking: the central figures shape the mass experience of everyone else around them, turning those others into an audience. To become a free individual one has to remake the social dream into one's own private movie.

The first few Hollywood movies Lang made also focus on the emergence of a kind of mass delusion, a social dream, but in these films nobody in particular, not even a superman, shapes that dream. Instead of manipulators, these movies focus on victims, who in effect are forced into the role of "star villain" by being falsely accused of notorious crimes. These victims try to escape their stardom, to become anonymous, but instead they are relentlessly pressed until their very efforts to escape drive them to become criminals. They desperately seek spaces the public cannot reach, but in these movies there is no safe private realm: the only available alternatives to the public arena are the realms of the divine or the degenerate, which blur together in these movies: the individual

110

warped by unfair accusations becomes both a figure of the crucified Christ and of a vicious animal snapping back when trapped.

Lang's movies investigate one of the paradoxes at the heart of individuality as presented in a mass medium: how can an entire audience appreciate a person who values being different from any "entire audience"? The fascist solution is, as we saw in the last chapter, the "folkish" belief in a superhuman cultural "personality": everyone gains a public face by identifying with the leader even though that leader seems to stand apart from everyone. The person who does not wish to join in this folkish unity is not then a free individual, but a person with no personality or a sinister manipulator, a cultureless Jew. Lang's German movies vacillate between the visible, rock-solid, unchanging face of the superhuman leader, and the invisible, unrecognizable face of the hidden manipulator. In *Metropolis*, we see this structure most completely laid out, with clear opposition between manipulation and leadership in the fight between Rotwang and Freder. The entire movie turns on the necessity of creating a visible body that the masses can believe in, though the movie stops short of the fascist conclusion that such a body must be a dictator. Instead, it creates a peculiar "mediator," a person whose function is simply to project, rather as a film does, the visions of the leaders into the minds of the masses.

In *M*, we see this system falling apart, as the one who is "projecting" into the mass mind is a deviant, Hans Beckert, who inserts tremendous emotion and movement into public consciousness. His projections do not give meaning to the order or provide him personal pleasure; instead they create chaos, which he experiences as self-torment. In this movie, leaders lose the mythic beauty of Lang's earlier films, becoming instead a sloppy, fat policeman (Lohmann) and a caricatured leather-clad criminal (Schränker). Even more disturbing than their failure to appear as heroes is that these leaders are completely devoted to the principle that routines must be kept in place: their role in society is to eliminate the one "nonmember," the one person who resists the usual rules (Beckert).

Though neither *M* nor *Metropolis* is fully in the fascist camp, both end up more on the collectivist side because they show that crowd actions are successful and that the individual can only be happy when a member of a crowd. In *Metropolis*, peace is restored by having a crowd of workers march up to the leaders, so that Freder can join the two groups together. In *M*, both the police and the criminals—the two collective organizations—succeed in finding the deviant child-murderer, though the process tears up the thoroughly designed social space—the criminals cut holes in doors and floors, while the police hide in Beckert's apartment in the dark. It is necessary to violate secure private spaces to remove deviance, but at least it can be removed. The last line of the movie, said by several mothers, is that they have to keep a closer watch on things, implying the need for a surveillance that cannot ever leave anyone alone.

In Lang's Hollywood movies, leadership is often presented as weak or "too late" to save the central figures from the distorting effects of mass beliefs. Persons try to lead or manipulate, but inevitably, the public responses they create escape their control and wreak havoc. Lang goes much further than the Hays Code in worrying about the effects of mass media: the Code describes crowds as lowering everyone's "moral mass resistance," while Lang presents crowds as unleashing everyone's criminal impulses. And insofar as movies create the crowd effect, they are implicated as causes of deviance. Lang seems distinctly aware of this contradiction in his early Hollywood films, and creates disturbing moments that undermine the entire operation of his narratives. *Fury* presents within its diegetic world a movie that appears to reveal that everyone, even the nicest and most ordinary people, are actually criminals waiting for an opportunity to commit crimes. The seeming recovery of morality at the end of *Fury* is contradicted by this movie-within-a-movie, so that the ending feels very much a Hollywood fantasy exposing itself as a fantasy. In *You Only Live Once*, the audience, thoroughly misled by Lang's use of movie conventions, joins the masses represented within the movie in reading clues as pointing to the guilt of the innocent main character, Eddie. While critics have treated this film as either flawed or partly avant-garde, I would suggest rather that it fits well with Lang's Hollywood themes, and is a version of a contradiction in numerous Hollywood films. David Bordwell comments that "the purpose of creating such an unreliable narration is evidently to compel the viewer to judge Eddie as unfairly as do all the respectable citizens. More generally, Lang's American films frequently construct a 'paranoid' spectator through a narration that brutally and abruptly manipulates point of view in order to conceal gaps and force the viewer to false conclusions."[3] Lang constructs misleading narration yet always reveals that we have been misled; he restores morality after we have joined characters on screen in following improper—or immoral—suggestions. Lang shows repeatedly that the triumph of morality over mass delusion, as required by the Hays Code, requires the triumph of movies over the power of movies themselves. The artificiality of his endings has to do with his deep understanding of the powerful contradiction inside movies: what grips audiences most powerfully is the mass experience of what is best kept out of the public eye. The feeling that his movies end falsely, I suggest, derives from the sense that they are betraying the movie experience itself. There is no good end to the turmoil that movies powerfully create.

Metropolis

One of Lang's movies, *Metropolis*, does end with an image of the crowd organized and tamed, and this is the movie that comes closest to endorsing a political philosophy, a fascism as fascism thinks of itself: benevolent, caring for the masses, uniting the whole social order. The movie was produced in 1927, five years after Mussolini founded a fascist regime in Italy and five years before Hitler came to power in Germany. The movie opens in the style of Soviet Montage, invoking Eisenstein and Vertov in its rhythmic motions of machinery and rhythmic shuffling of workers. There is a feeling of revolution waiting to happen, as the workers seem herded together like animals. As in Eisenstein, we await the organic, fluid, natural alternative to the mechanical, entrapping geometry. Lang does turn to an organic, fluid world, but in a disturbing image of decadence: the movie shifts to an upper-class garden, with curving fountains of water through which we watch lovers cavort. The garden scene is shot in classic Hollywood shot/reverse shot, with most of the focus on one male and one female. Instead of seeming organic and natural, as the shots of waves do in Eisenstein films, Lang gives us a sense of this garden as a perverse version of Hollywood.

The contrast between the two classes is thus a contrast between two filmic styles and, we might say, two political philosophies. The rest of the movie strives to unite these opposed visions, to find a way to unite the broad geometries of mass life with the intimate exchange of looks of personal life. This effort to unite the two worlds and the two film styles begins with the interruption of the climactic Hollywood kiss in the upper-class garden: as the hero, Freder, bends to kiss, he looks over at an elevator door, which is too tall and covered with diagonal lines, a design that does not fit with the fluid fountains and is reminiscent of the opening diagonals. The door opens and a crowd of ragged children come in, led by Maria: thus the first event that sets the plot in motion is the irruption into the world of Hollywood upper-class love scenes elements from the "collectivist" style of filmmaking: the intrusion of the crowd, the working class, into the upper class.

113

Maria and Freder exchange intense glances, and we know that she is the true love he should pursue rather than the decadent woman he was about to kiss, but instead of any personal interaction, Maria says, "Look, these are your brothers": in effect, she redirects his look at her, and implies what becomes clear in the rest of the movie, that, in this film, to achieve the look of love, the look that is the climax of the Hollywood plot, the man has to look not at the woman directly but at her through a vision of the crowd. The rest of the movie he spends earning the right to kiss her by becoming a brother with the workers and gaining the vision of the crowd. We could say he discovers his culture, his unity with the people, escaping the individualism and isolation and ignorance of the decadent upper-class world—and as a result he gains a better form of love than he seemed to have in that decadent world. In a sense, the movie implies that he has to leave the style of Hollywood movies to achieve the goal of Hollywood plots—a love affair that is "in tune" with the masses and with the theater audience.

When Maria leaves, Freder follows her and ends up in a "middle realm" between the upper- and lower-class worlds. The sequence that occurs here becomes a kind of mix of the two film styles that defined upper and lower worlds in that we have a shot/reverse shot structure as in the upper-class scene of love, but in this case the "reverse shot" to Freder's face is an image of complex diagonals of machinery akin to the opening montage: in other words, we have a shot/reverse shot between a person and a vast machine. What happens as he watches in effect suggests a way out of the opposed styles: the machinery turns into a face looking back at him as he looks at it. The movie is setting up what it will show for the rest of the film, that a human body, a face, must replace the inhuman geometry as the image of entire system. But not, of course, the horrible face of Moloch, which appears in this scene as a monster eating the workers; instead Freder must become this public image, so that the workers and the masters see him instead of seeing the alienating mechanical geometry when they try to visualize the entire system. Freder's body must become an image of the collective.

For that to occur, Freder has to learn to look at the masses the way Maria does, and essentially substitute his face for hers, because hers is the face to which the masses respond. Maria's role in the early part of the movie is to prepare the workers to accept Freder instead of her as the face to believe. She does this by performing a religious ceremony deep under the city in front of multiple crosses, an image which would resonate with the root word of fascism, "fasces," meaning a bundle of sticks:

114

Maria's goal is to create a society bound tightly together, as fascism will later also seek.

Maria prepares the workers to accept a new leader by telling them a tale of Babel, a story of workers and leaders separated by lack of communication. Maria ends saying they need a "mediator," someone to put the dream of the leaders into the minds of the workers; in other words, she is advocating a dream-industry embodied in a media-maker who can provide the medium for transmitting the dream into all the mass minds (we should not make much of the pun in English between "mediator" and "media" because it does not work in German). Her speech is represented as itself a movie playing in the workers' minds: she is the first representation of a filmmaker within this film, someone who is creating the mass consciousness that will allow a leader to operate.

Watching Maria present her "movie" to the workers are two other possible "filmmakers": Freder and his father. The movie becomes a contest between these two in creating the image that will be presented to the workers as a replacement for Maria. The father enlists the aid of a scientist, Rotwang, to create a technological copy of Maria to mislead the workers. Rotwang's methodology is presented very much as the transformation of the flesh-and-blood Maria into a movie image. He first captures Maria by projecting a beam of light on her: putting her in the spotlight, transforming her from a filmmaker into a kind of star, and thereby wrests the process of projection away from her.

Rotwang does not quite gain control over Maria: he cannot bring her to do and say what he wants. Instead, he creates a technological copy of her by transferring her image onto a generic metallic female body. This process of putting her image onto the animatronic body involves lights surrounding the body while a kind of glowing liquid flows from Maria into the body and eventually becomes a heart pumping inside it, from which flows a circulatory system of light. Then this image of the internal system of flowing light disappears as the robot becomes the exact copy of Maria. The process thus creates an image of Maria not photographically, but by creating electrical versions of heart and blood, which automatically then generate the physical copy of her entire body. What is being copied is not simply Maria's physicality, but the "blood and heart" which symbolize her power to unite the workers. In a sense, he is capturing her filmmaking ability, the flow of light emerging from her heart.

The false Maria uses the power she has borrowed from the real Maria to first incite the upper-class males to become a many-eyed monster by dancing a very curvy and sinuous dance (figs. 21, 22, and 23).

Figs. 21–23. The False Maria's dancing . . .

causes spectators . . .

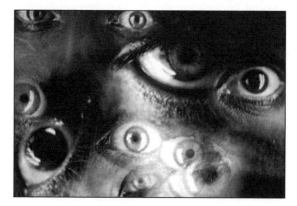

to merge into a collective monster.

The upper class dissolves into a riot of male aggression, fighting with each other and then wildly dancing with women. Then the false Maria goes to the workers and incites them to riot and destroy the machines that run this whole society, a strange tactic never fully explained, but it seems to aim at having the workers accept repressive measures in the name of restoring order. In effect, the transformation of Maria into the robot copy alters the nature of her influence on those who listen to her: what was a political message becomes instead a distorted sexual message, so that even when it speaks the language of politics it leads only to chaos. In effect, Rotwang's science does just what Hollywood aims at in its Hays Code: turning politics into sexuality.

The moment of recovery by workers and by leaders is the moment of saying, "Where is your son?"—rather close to a Hays Code solution. At the moment of perverse mass reactions, of immorality which is both sexual and politically rebellious, the answer is familial morality. However, in this movie familial morality does not operate by bringing everyone to turn their attention away from the mass gathering and focus instead on images of private life, as it would in a Hollywood movie. Rather, this movie presents a mass familial morality that replaces the mass sexuality that threatened to overturn everything. The first step of this saving of the social order occurs when Freder and Maria save the children by getting them all to gather on a huge gong, which looks like a giant breast: Freder and Maria begin acting as the parents of the entire social order, particularly of the workers. The workers are told, "Freder has saved your children," and this becomes the promise of his leadership: he will make the overall social relationship of classes into familial relationships.

Note how this restoration of family differs from Hollywood's images: it is not the mass riot breaking up as each family returns to its own private space; rather the mass riot itself is transformed into a mass family, as we see at the end when the workers and masters join together in ritual at the cathedral that climaxes in a handshake, that symbol of friendship or personal bond. This final handshake occurs between the foreman, leader of the workers, and Frederson, leader of the upper classes. Freder, playing the role of mediator, brings the two hands together and then steps out of the way. He does not become the leader himself. I suggest that this small detail suggests the role of the film and filmmakers: Freder becomes the image through which the two classes in this divided society look to see each other. He then steps aside to let them physically connect. Freder becomes the right kind of filmmaker, creating the consciousness in everyone else that allows the social order to function.

Freder's role as mediator is entwined throughout the movie with his role as lover of Maria. Their love is not simply a parallel to the uniting of the classes: rather it is causally related to the social structure. Freder only gains her love by learning to love the masses, and he only brings the masses and leaders to unite after he finally loves (and kisses) Maria. Their love for each other is in some mysterious way derived from and a source of the love that unites the social classes. The movie thus follows the usual Hollywood notion that riots are due to bad sexuality and social harmony due to true love, but I would still argue that it is closer to collectivist ideology than to Hollywood individualism. The riot of bad sexuality in this movie is what severs the crowd into separate individual bodies, while the effect of the restoration of love is to create the geometrically organized crowd that stands as an image of collectivist order. In other words, the movie reverses the logic of Hollywood's intertwining of sexuality and politics. In Hollywood films, misguided sexuality produces collectivist action; proper sexuality brings the crowd to a vision of private life, which is then pursued by individuals separately. In this movie, bad sexuality sets people against each other, and good love brings them into a mass body.

The movie is full of the sort of imagery that was crucial to Nazi rhetoric, in particular the sense that there is something like "blood" that unites everyone, which appears both in the fluid light that flows through the veins of the false Maria and in the liquid that threatens to drown everything when the workers riot. The movie suggests that the social order depends on properly containing and channeling a liquid flowing through the veins of the whole social order. Also, Rotwang is presented in terms that make him close to what Hitler would describe as the Jew, as Peter Dolgenos and John Tulloch have argued.[4] Rotwang lives in a small house isolated from everyone else with a mysterious star upon it; that star is identified in Von Harbou's novel version of *Metropolis* as the "seal of Solomon" (Von Harbou, *Metropolis* 43). Rotwang creates a false image of the ideal German: the false Maria is an alien "passing" for a citizen. The notion that culture has to be defended against such disguised aliens is a crucial Nazi trope.

M

The movie most often called Lang's masterpiece, *M*, released two years before Hitler came to power, focuses intently on the need to uncover a hidden "alien" whose presence is deforming and degrading the whole culture. When a leather-clad leader describes the child-murderer as a "nonmember," the fears that led to fascism are strongly evoked. In this movie, though, the problem is identifying the "nonmember." As the title indicates, *M* is a movie about marks that identify people, the writing that the social order performs upon the body of the individual in order to give it a distinct role. Or perhaps we should say it is about reading, the reading of the individual body performed by various kinds of gazes—the personal gaze of the family, the regulatory gaze of officials, and the anonymous gaze of strangers and crowds. The movie seems to start by directing our attention to the family and the criminal's disruption of it, as we watch Elsie Beckmann's mother call her name across an empty courtyard as Elsie is at that moment being taken away and killed by the child-murderer. But though the family is invoked, what we see of it are only plates on tables, washlines, hallways, stairs, and children meeting parents on the street: we see the external trappings and setting of the family, but we do not see the family in operation. Instead, we see a "familial" inter-action between Hans and his victim, who is drawn to her death by his acting in a "familiar" way—asking to be called "uncle" and buying her a balloon. In a sense, then, the opening of the movie sets up the notion that familial interactions are not really "personal" at all, but rather follow a code involving certain kinds of spaces, certain words and tones of voice and gestures, all of which can be imitated by complete strangers. The image of Elsie's death is her balloon caught in power lines, an "intimate" object in the wrong setting, held not by a child's hand but by an utterly impersonal social structure. Hans's crime is in effect the alienation of the familial from its human and social setting. His acts threaten to expose the impersonality of what appears personal, or the transferability of the personal to impersonal spaces.

One of the strongest effects of this movie is the presentation of social spaces as cut up into inhospitable shapes: we see banisters, clotheslines, doorframes, all disrupting open spaces and making it difficult for people to do what they want to do. The goal of liberal society—to provide each family with a private space that allows the people to freely pursue their private goal—has gone haywire in this movie. There are no private houses seen anywhere: everyone lives in an apartment surrounded by fences and banistered staircases that seem to cut up or make awkward the semiprivate spaces of each family. The scenes of parents picking up children after school emphasize that families have to pass through public spaces to connect to their own children, and in those public spaces families break up. Similarly, the scenes of friends becoming angry and accusatory as they smoke their pipes and discuss the murders show the breakdown of the classic interpersonal space of dinner conversation: there is no trust that one's private space can be shared by others at all. The shot/reverse shot of Hollywood films, the paradigmatic center of interpersonal relations in eyes looking into eyes, is parodied in two early sequences: a small man on the street is accused by a large man of being the child-murderer, and we see each from the other's point of view, in an extremely alienating exchange of looks. A bit later, two witnesses confront each other with their opposed testimony about the color of a hat, and we again see direct point-of-view shots reversing, so that both men are looking directly into the camera and almost spitting in anger at each other. One-to-one interaction is not the way to get to "know" someone at all: it produces error and mistaken identification. The basis of the liberal order is threatened by this failure of one-to-one interactions to reveal the truth.

The movie devotes almost all its time to relationships that are formal and social, not private and personal. Probably the friendliest relationship we watch is that between the police and the thief Franz, who is caught after the criminals have captured the child-murderer Hans Beckert. The police know Franz and they manipulate their intimacy to get him to violate his relationship with the other criminals. Essentially every scene of interactions among what would seem to be friends ends in an argument or a deception or a routine, such as picking up children after school. The only time a person reveals much about himself as a person is at the end when Beckert makes his speech about his crime, and that is a speech about how he is split, how he pursues himself, how he never feels comfortably alone except immediately after killing a child.

Beckert is not then an anomaly that wrecks temporarily the intimate, liberal order of private families; rather he is in effect a logical outcome of a social order that has been badly divided into private spaces: everyone is divided like Beckert, internally split into a "self" and a surveying public eye. When Beckert finally explains what seems to him the reason for committing his crime, his explanation becomes an analysis of what we have been watching throughout the movie, the sense of being continually observed and judged. The intense surveillance that succeeds in locating Beckert simply makes visible another surveillance that he has felt all his life:

I have no control over this evil thing inside me, the fire, the voices, the torment . . . following me, silently, but I can feel it there . . . It's me, pursuing myself . . . I want to escape, escape from myself!

But it's impossible . . . I can't escape. I have to obey it. I have to
run . . . endless streets . . . I want to escape, to get away, and I'm
pursued by ghosts. Ghosts of mothers, and of those children . . .
They never leave me . . . They are there, always there . . . Always,
except when I do it . . . Then I can't remember anything. (ellipses
in the original)

He kills, then, to halt the ghosts of mothers and children pursuing him,
ghosts which are part of himself pursuing himself. In other words, he
kills to escape the social implications of his own desires. His killing is not
presented, then, as the "expression" of a desire to have some kind of
interaction with children, some kind of pleasure from killing; rather it is
an act performed to silence the crowd of voices condemning him. He
kills to be free of the unintended and unavoidable social judgments that
accompany every act of an individual.

Social judgments are in a sense public readings of the acts of individuals, and Beckert kills to silence such readings. His first appearance follows
a scene of a crowd reading a poster describing his murders. After they
finish, his shadow falls across the poster as he starts out after a new victim.
At first this seems to be the coming-to-life of the murderer just described
in print, but after we hear Beckert's explanation at the end of the movie,
we can reinterpret this first appearance: Beckert's shadow falls across the
poster as he sets out to kill again because he is trying to black out the
words written on walls about him, to silence the crowds of people talking
about him. He is at war with those words. His writing to the newspaper
in the midst of his killings to claim that he will not stop does not contradict this: it is not so much that he wants publicity, but that publicity
about him is in effect the cause of his acts. He kills because he has been
made public as a monster, and only after such killing can he have silence.
Perhaps the silence after a killing is the experience of no longer feeling
split between public and private images—at that moment he is precisely
what people think he is, a murderer.

Beckert's act is an effort to separate the social world and its way of
reading him from his own acts of writing. It is impossible, precisely because writing, expressing, knowing oneself only occurs through the use
of the socially provided symbols and spaces. Those socially provided
symbols and spaces work, recent literary theory has argued, by dividing
up the continuous field of experience (or space or feeling): the divisions
make the acts of individuals readable, make movement into acts, into
expression and not merely part of the general flow of everything. The

act of expression, the desire to be oneself and not divided from oneself, is impossible, because the very act of expression is an act of dividing up what emerges from a person so that it can be read by others—and so it becomes something that others can read in ways one did not intend. The movie goes further than literary theory: it is not just that symbols are arbitrary, but that the act of expression requires physical acts which betray "meanings" to public readers through what might seem utterly accidental qualities of the physical action. In this movie, what turns out to be most revealing about Beckert's letters to the paper is not the deep psychological traits which some graphologist claims to discover (and which are described rather amusingly while Beckert makes faces at himself in the mirror), but rather the mere color of the lead he uses—red, which leaves a residue on the shelf where he writes and so reveals he has been there. Similarly, the most important quality about the title letter "M" is that it is produced in chalk and thus is loose and dusty and can be transferred to Beckert's back by a beggar falling against him. "M" obviously does symbolically stand for "murderer" but any mark would do as well. It is not the symbolic form of the letter but its ability to be accidentally transferred to a surface on which it was not directly "written" that gives it its value. Writing, the act of trying to "express" or communicate, carries utterly accidental physical consequences, which may be more "readable" than the symbolic structure of the writing itself.

The search for Beckert is precisely a search for accidental physical residues that accompany acts. The police never find blood or knives: they find cigarette papers and grains of candy. The movie suggests that a continual surveillance of such insignificant marks is the only way to eliminate the deviance which Beckert represents. However, if we take Beckert's own description of his acts, it is this surveillance that is producing persons like Beckert. The movie goes further than merely giving us Beckert's words to suggest that it is the detailed structuring of the social order that produces his acts by showing us the interconnection between the lines criss-crossing the whole social order and his compulsion in the second scene of his pursuing a child.

In this second scene, we are following along, looking over his shoulder as it were, and we get to see the compulsion first come upon him. He is looking in a window of a cutlery store, in which there is a square mirror hanging at a 45 degree angle, framed by hundreds of table knives arranged in parallel lines, creating a complex diamond shape above radiating fans of spoons below the mirror. In that mirror, in the center of this complex array of geometric shapes, there appears an image of a girl, which sparks his desire to kill. His compulsion thus appears in the middle of an array of lines created by domestic objects, an array of knives that are typically considered "not dangerous" and therefore useful in creating the safe, secure domestic scene of eating.

The array of repeated shapes even bears resemblance to the designs of a Busby Berkeley musical, with one girl in the middle of repeated shapes all around. The girl appears then as the central element in a dazzling display of pleasant domestic life: the movie implies that Beckert's compulsion is in some way intertwined with the complex and overly-designed domestic world. Furthermore, the vision of the girl is doubly mediated by two pieces of glass (window and mirror)—or even triply mediated, since the reflection passes through the window glass twice, once from the girl to the mirror and once from the mirror to Beckert. Several features of the shot highlight the sense that he is having a mediated vision, that he has to look through quite a bit to see this child. The window includes various reflections of its own as well as those of the mirror behind it, faint images of people passing across the girl and across Beckert's reflection—images of the ghosts he describes as pursuing him everywhere. As he turns to follow the girl, his image becomes doubled with a very distinct reflection in the window (not in the mirror) which moves in parallel to his "real body," so that what have been passing ghostly images turn into a single image that moves exactly as he moves. The scene enacts what he described in the speech, ghosts surrounding him that are revealed to be a second self—and he acts to eliminate this second self (figs. 24 and 25).

We might say then that what happens when he sees the girl is that he realizes he has to escape from the lines and the pursuing ghosts: he has to kill what is haunting him, his second self. When the girl appears, he is driven to escape from the regulated world of shop windows, proper mealtimes, parents, and normal judgments. When Beckert cannot get to the girl because her mother appears, he is then flung into a world full of even more aggressive lines that cut across him—first another store window with a rotating spiral, then a bush behind which he sits to drink to recover. The fact that we see him through that bush is not a result of his hiding: he is in a public restaurant, but just filmed through a bush. We could say that this shot suggests he is entrapped by his perverse desire, but what we see is that he feels trapped because he has failed to enact his perverse desire: the killing would have released him from the sense of entrapment, but having failed, he drinks as a weak secondary way to escape.

Figs. 24–25. Framing a victim . . .

splits the subject into self and murderer.

We too as viewers find ourselves caught up in the complex designs pursuing Beckert. In the beginning, the movie seems to be about the horror of killing a child, and we join with everyone in seeking to remove the horror. But when we see him, he seems rather innocuous as we follow him about, and we are caught up instead in the complexities of the search for him, gradually coming to a rather different horror: the horror of living in a society that can pursue and observe everyone and persecute them endlessly. If at first society is unfree because of the possible threat of Beckert everywhere (and of anyone at all being Beckert), it then comes to seem unfree because there are hidden people observing and judging everywhere. So the movie gives us in two different ways the experience of paranoia.

The paranoia that is the fear of Beckert is easily identified with the motivation for Nazism: hunt out and eliminate all deviants. When Nazism was firmly in power, this movie was used as an example of the evils Jews bring: in the supposed documentary, *The Eternal Jew*, Beckert's speech about his compulsions is presented as an example of a Jew making excuses for his evils. Goebbels even claimed that the film was proto-Nazi. Tom Gunning argues that "Goebbels's claim . . . is no more inherently convincing than later claims that the film is anti-Nazi. Kracauer himself recognized the ambiguity of the film, wavering between different attitudes."[5]

Lang certainly seems to be evoking Nazis in his representation of Schränker, the leader of the gang which finally captures Beckert. Schränker is clothed in a "leather jacket and cane [which] summon up the image of an SS officer," according to Gunning.[6] Schränker describes the child-killer in terms reminiscent of Hitler's description of Jews: "This monster has no right to live. He must disappear! He must be eliminated, without pity, without scruples." Schränker is presented as coldly logical, and the most chilling description of Beckert is his statement that the child-killer is simply a "nonmember." The phrase would seem to refer to the society of criminals, but it suggests that Beckert is outside all forms of social organization. Schränker starts the discussion by establishing himself as the representative of a highly organized business: "I confirm according to regulations . . . the leadership of every organization in our union is represented . . . You are authorized to vote on behalf of your members . . . Some nonmember is screwing up . . . interfering with our business." Everything "normal" in this movie is highly structured—and Beckert is driven to escape structure, thereby becoming a "nonmember" of the entire social body.

In *Metropolis* and *M*, one senses the need for a total organization of the social order: one cannot let every person go their own way, cannot conceive of the social order as a set of free spaces with minimal overall organization. *Metropolis* suggests a necessary overarching structure (head, hands, heart) so that the social system is one body with organically related parts. *M* suggests the presence of all kinds of structures that shape human relations; it hints that those structures get in the way of humans, divide them, force them into positions they don't want, and haunt them, but the only escape is to be a "nonmember" and essentially become nonexistent (a nonmember is like something that is not a part of a body, a limb that is not a member). In both movies, the question of the role of "heart," of caring and kindness and human connection, to the social structure, is raised, but in *M* there is no easy answer about what is the "kind" way to treat everyone. While making *M*, Lang may have been losing his belief in the fascist social order surrounding him; soon after finishing the film, he left Germany to start a new career as a Hollywood filmmaker.

Fury and *You Only Live Once*

When Lang arrived in Hollywood the first movie he made, *Fury*, repeats, but inverts, many of the themes of *M*. The movie was first going to be called "Mob Rule."[7] Once again, there is a maniac on the loose who assaults young women, and once again there is a mob that hunts down someone they have identified as the maniac. On the hunt, the mob breaks into a building, then a locked cell within the building, as the mob did in *M*, yet, in this case, their target is innocent, and the crowd is presented as a lynch mob. Lang seems to have inverted his politics: now the individual is threatened by the deviant social order, not the social order by the deviant individual. Joe Wilson, the hero in *Fury*, summarizes the theme: "they won't let you . . . live right." The movie follows good Hollywood plotting in starting with a happy couple, then inserting a crowd that threatens that couple, and finally having the couple united at the end as they finally escape the crowd.

However, the movie does as much to undermine standard Hollywood themes as it does to promote them. While the movie ends with the couple kissing, there is left little sense of the innocent individual: we have seen that the nicest, most ordinary people contain within them impulses to commit murder and mayhem. It is not enough to simply leave people alone: there need to be safeguards against these murderous

126

impulses. Much is made of the failure of the governor to send the national guard when the mob first threatened the jail: federal military forces are necessary to control the impulses in the sweetest citizens of little towns. But far more disturbing is the transformation wrought in the hero of this movie, Joe Wilson, a "Joe Doe" ordinary fellow: he turns into a monster, a leader of a vicious gang, as he sets out to get revenge for the lynching that the citizens of Strand tried to perform on him. Within the nicest, sweetest couple, there are murderous impulses that can be unleashed by the wrong social setting.

Lang pursued a similar set of issues in his next Hollywood movie, *You Only Live Once*. We follow a happy couple as they are hounded by false public opinions, and once again the pressure leads the hero to eventually commit a crime akin to the one he was falsely accused of. These movies explore the distortions introduced into private individuals and public opinion when there is no overarching order to shape mass opinion. We see serious misjudgment of the individual for a good part of the movie, and the effect of that public pressure is to warp the individual. The innocence of the heroes in *Fury* and in *You Only Live Once* does not last beyond the false accusations. Still, the difference between Hollywood and protocollectivist Weimar can be seen quite clearly in the feelings we end up with in these movies: in *Fury* and *You Only Live Once*, we feel mostly that the mass emotions should never have become active, while in the Weimar movies we end up hoping for mass action under an effective regime to control deviance.

In *Fury*, there is a peculiar way that the stories of private life and public opinion are connected. Certain kinds of expectations in one realm end up being realized in twisted form in the other in such a way that it feels as if there is a strange narrative logic tying them together. In particular, the movie is built on a gradually increasing rhythm that seems to lead to the climactic embrace of the lovers, but in the middle of the film the story switches from their private lives to a very public realm while the rhythm continues to build, so that it seems as if the desires and forces in one realm are simply continuing to grow transplanted into the other. Thus, Joe and Katherine begin the movie by separating after looking at a marriage bed and talking quite intimately. The movie then enters a montage of waiting, a series of cross-cut scenes of each of them living their separate lives but increasingly feeling frustrated as Joe tries to make enough money for them to live together. Finally, he writes to her saying he has enough, and both begin traveling toward each other. The cross-cutting continues as the two approach, but then another story erupts as

Joe is stopped by a deputy and falsely accused of a crime. The cross-cutting between the two of them switches to a series of quadruple cross-cuts, with scenes of the sheriff and the townspeople gathering in a bar to become a mob intercut with shots of Joe and Katherine, he in jail, she on the road. The rhythm of delay and growing impatience starts up again, but this time with greater intensity and now includes the frustration of the crowd as they anticipate a hanging and the frustration of the sheriff as he waits for state troops to hold off the mob. The climax of all this is then not the meeting of Joe and Katherine, but rather the contact between Joe and the townspeople as they riot and invade the prison.

Even as the riot erupts, the story of Joe and Katherine coming together continues to build, so that Katherine arrives just as the jail is being blown up: she faints as she sees what seems to be Joe being killed.

The attack on the jail thus seems the climax of the delayed sexual union, and numerous details further create that sense. Precisely as the townspeople are heaving a large log against the jail door, the movie has a cut to Katherine on the road shouting, "No, No," to passing cars as she tries to flag a ride. Her "no" seems then an answer to the people trying to break into the prison, and their act then has much the spirit of violating a woman (as the phallic log suggests as well). That the whole act of breaking in goes from a log breaking down a door to fire and an explosion inside the prison mirrors the physical details of sexuality—penetration, heat, explosion that reaches the center. The destruction of Joe is the climax of all the frustration of waiting to be married.

Much about the rising passion of the townspeople suggests as well that they are acting on sexual motives. The final line that moves them to start down the street from the bar is a taunt from a man: "What kind of eggs are you, soft-boiled, that you won't protect a girl?" By rioting, the men escape this accusation of softness and impotence. As they travel down the street, we see a heavy-set man with two women on his arm: this riot provides an aura of masculine prowess unavailable in daily life. Before the riot, a barber speaks of impulses that are nearly irresistible, claiming everyone has them and illustrating it with his impulse to cut a man's throat while shaving him. Such impulses are all in essence "lusts," as the governor describes the riot as a "brutal outburst of lust for vengeance."

We too in the audience are given a sense of impulses toward violence within us: as the crowd approaches the police station, we are placed within the crowd, with stones even coming over our head from behind. Martial music plays and we recognize the thrill of joining in this mob. At this point, though, we resist, identifying with Joe. We feel then a tide of frustration as the mob slowly approaches the prison, and this tide of frustration continues what was set up by the long opening montages: we want something to happen. Our desire for excitement, for a climax, set up by the rhythms of the whole movie, lead to a hope that the innocent Joe will make some sort of heroic act to resist the crowd. Our desire for a climactic expression of the desire for freedom is in part a desire for some kind of violent release, and in that sense gives us the same feeling motivating the crowd.

Instead of seeing Joe's heroic escape, Lang misleads us at the climax: we are made to believe that Joe is killed in the explosion, so we end up feeling as Katherine's and Joe's brothers feel—that a terrible crime has been committed. When Joe returns, we are shocked and thoroughly set up to join his desire for revenge. From then on, the movie inverts its earlier classification of Joe and of the mob of townspeople: he was innocent, they impulsively criminal; now he becomes impulsively criminal and they become more and more presented as innocent persons. Joe even creates a "mob" with his two brothers, talking of his plans for revenge as similar to what gangsters do. So the "mob" mentality switches from the crowd to Joe.

The movie shows that every person has two opposed personalities, depending on whether they are in their private lives or have been swept up by a mob. Katherine tries to use this shift in personality to say that the townspeople are not responsible for their actions: "They're not murderers, they're part of a mob—a mob doesn't think." But Joe, part of his mob with his brothers, also does not think, and so sets out to get revenge for the other mob's desire to murder him. Both the townspeople and Joe become killers because they believe they have identified other persons as murderers.

The movie thus raises the question of what we in the audience are going to do: are we going to become a mob, excited by violence and motivated by believing we can identify other persons as murderers? The movie presents this question directly, when Joe says,

> I've been in a movie, watching a newsreel of myself getting burned alive . . . They like it, they get a kick out of seeing a man get burned alive—a big kick—what an explosion—it blew the cell door off.

We in the movie audience also are looking to get a "big kick" out of seeing a movie version of a man burned alive. Our desire for a big kick is made more acceptable because we experience it as a desire shared by all in the crowd around us, not as an individual motive. The people in the town also experience this power of the crowd to alter their desires. Lang highlights the transformative power of crowds and of movies by including in the trial a movie, taken by a journalist, that reveals the supposedly innocent townspeople performing criminally violent acts with great glee as part of the mob rioting. The movie within this movie reveals the thrill of participating in lustful acts, and we in the audience can similarly enjoy the thrill of watching other people get exposed as having such lustful behavior. The scenes of the people grinning as they riot in effect give people in that town the experience we might have if cameras were turned on us as we watch this movie: we experience pleasure in the horrible deeds performed by those townspeople, and we want as they do release from the frustrating rhythm of delay that permeates ordinary life.

In Lang's next movie, *You Only Live Once*, he goes much further to draw the movie audience into the excitement and quick decision-making of violent moments, to bring the audience to share the mass opinion that produces the crimes at the center of the story: first, to condemn an innocent man, and then to drive that innocent man to commit a version of the very crime he is falsely accused of. Lang uses the structures of narrative, the movement of rhythms that build a sense of frustration, and then the almost automatic, emotional connections we make between scenes at the violent climax of that rhythm, to lead us to our wrong conclusions. We watch the main character Eddie increasingly get frustrated as he tries to hold a job, and we watch as he is asked to join a criminal activity: we too feel a sense of frustration and hope that something would happen to break the tight grip of Eddie's suffering. We view his possible return to crime with dread, but with that fascination of possible release from the frustration of "going nowhere" with him. Then we suddenly cut to a violent explosion, a crime in progress, that seems to be the next logical step in Eddie's story, and the camera moves in to show us a hat with Eddie's initials in its band, a hat we have seen before and know is his. The normal reading of the story leads us to conclude that Eddie is part of this crime.

Critics such as George Wilson and Tom Gunning have found the manipulation of narrative structures in this movie a break with the standard practice of Hollywood movies.[8] However, as I argued in Chapter 1, much the same thing goes on in *Young Mr. Lincoln*, when we are manipulated to believe that one of the two brothers accused of murder must be guilty, and we are similarly manipulated in *Fury* to believe Joe is dead. I suggest that such moments are actually quite common; indeed they are relatively necessary to allow for surprise twists and to increase the suspense of thrillers. What is most interesting about the movies I am considering is that they directly turn on themselves as movies and thereby illustrate what I have argued the Hays Code states: that movies will always dangerously mislead people and so have to have morality imposed upon them artificially. The moral ending of Hollywood movies always has a certain element of undermining the very spirit of movies themselves. The basic effects of filmmaking as the Hays Code envisions them—turning each audience into an immoral mob—have to be countered by the assertion of the morality of the purpose to which this mob is assembled.

In *You Only Live Once* and *Young Mr. Lincoln*, young men are falsely accused of crimes and the audience is set up to believe they did those crimes. In both movies, there is a surprising revelation of truth. In *Young Mr. Lincoln*, the dangers of false opinion are avoided by Lincoln's clever arguments, but in *You Only Live Once* the dangers are not avoided, for the falsely accused young man, Eddie, so tormented that he believes the accusations will never end, actually commits a crime just when he could be proven innocent. The final effort to convince Eddie involves a person who has had a personal relationship to him—a priest. But this attempt to break through Eddie's distrust of public voices backfires, as Eddie shoots the priest. The sympathetic priest then sacrifices himself, concealing from the authorities that he has been shot in order to atone for the public's crime against Eddie. Eddie's story revolves around crimes of misreading: the public misreads the evidence of the bank robbery; he misreads the warden and the priest's words. When Eddie's misreading leads him to be as guilty as he has falsely been portrayed, there is then no way out of the false opinions. This movie leaves no way to return to a trusted reality. So there is a certain logic to the strange ending of this movie, when it steps beyond "realism" entirely: Eddie, shot, looks into a wooded scene, and sees the trees getting brighter in an eerie way and then hears the priest's voice saying, "You are free, Eddie, you are free." The ending remains thoroughly ambiguous—is this Eddie going to heaven, going to hell, having an hallucination as he dies, or what? Is it in Eddie's mind or not?

In *Fury*, there is a variant of this unrealistic moment. When Joe walks the streets after rejecting Katherine's ultimatum that, knowing all he has done, she will leave him if he does not turn himself in, he sees in shop windows ghostly figures of the townspeople who will die, and when he runs away, eerie lighting and sounds suggest that someone is following him. If he follows out his plan, he will be forever haunted by images that will terrify him. Reality has been distorted by his acts, and he will then live in a distorted reality. His speech at the end is an effort to restore reality, but as he says, this act cannot restore anyone's belief in the nation or the public or what enters public consciousness: morality and truth cannot be part of public consciousness, though they can rather magically be asserted at the ends of movies.

In Lang's third Hollywood movie, *You and Me*, he finally manages to unite an overarching vision of the American social system and a love story, but we can see how difficult he finds this task by the strange shifts in genre within what is otherwise a fairly ordinary story. The movie seeks to establish that the American social structure does not produce "mob psychology" by contrasting two "musical" numbers: first, one about the world of a department store (representing the American system), then one about the world of gangs (representing a system ruled by dictatorial figures). The movie begins with a montage musical number in which a voice-over sings the message that you need money to get what you want as we move throughout a department store, from its neon marquee through a series of consumer items punctuated with images of a cash register being rung up. This opening number is a variant of the opening style of *Metropolis*, a rhythmic exploration of the mechanical structure of a social institution. The city in *Metropolis* is formed of jagged buildings but it is made to pulse by a system of turbines and dynamos, engines that pump "fluid" through the city architecture. In *You and Me*, a department store is brought to life by cash registers that pump money through the economic pipelines that connect the store to private homes. As in *Metropolis*, no people are shown in the opening montage, so we are left with the same question: is this system one that entraps people or one that frees people? The refrain of the opening musical number, "You have to pay," sounds quite ominous, and ends up reverberating throughout the movie in disturbing ways because the main characters are all ex-convicts and we hear much discussion of what they have to give up until they have fully paid their debt to society. It is not merely objects that one cannot fully have until one has paid; it is marriage partners as well, as the judicial system in this film declares that until done with their parole, ex-cons are not allowed to marry.

Contrasting with the opening montage's emphasis on properly paying for everything, including one's love life, a second montage consists of a weird nostalgic group memory of being in prison together, with a different refrain: "You can't go it alone." The two montages represent two opposed ways of creating social cohesion. In the old system, people feel secure only when they are supported by group membership, in the new when they have a clear position in the social order, which provides them the money to pay for things. Being able to pay does not mean one is removed from all groups, but rather that one has been inserted into a vast system of distribution of things and people.

The opening montage represents modernity, the high-tech store, with its division not only of labor but of the "departments" of everyday life (sports, clothes, bedding, etc.). By dividing up all the pieces of everyday life, a bewildering array of seemingly different private lives is possible while everyone is channeled into a coherent social structure: individuality becomes choosing a set of market niches that define one. Instead of total loyalty to one gang and one "big shot," one has multiple loyalties: to one's private family, one's "department," one's boss, and one's co-workers. This social system does not provide a totalizing experience of group consciousness, but rather multiple smaller emotional satisfactions.

The main plot of the movie shows events which lead the hero, Joe Dennis, to rejoin his gang, a choice he makes when he realizes he has been deceived by his wife, Mary, who never told him that she is an ex-con just as he is. His feeling that his private life has been based on fraud leads him back to the gang, which then attempts to rob the department store where he and his wife work. That robbery fails because Mary has turned them in, so that as the gang enters the store, they encounter the owner and guards. The owner does not, however, send them to prison (which would in the terms of the movie be leaving them in the world of gangs, since the musical dream of the old social order was set in prison). Instead, the gang members are given an arithmetic lesson by Mary. She creates a balance sheet for the robbery that shows that mob action literally does not pay as well as working in a store. What begins as one giant payoff—the crime that would take $40,000 of goods all at once—ends up divided into such small amounts for each person that it is less than the accumulated small hourly wages each person would have received by working. The logic of the arithmetic lesson is rather precisely the replacement of the ethos of collectivist thought with the ethos of individualism. Collectivist thought argues that when individuals join together, each one gets in a sense the whole value of the entire group deposited in his or her "emotional" bank account. In a sense, that would imply that each robber would get the whole $40,000, at least as an emotional satisfaction. Mary's argument is that each one gets only a small piece of that large experience.

133

Mary's arithmetic lesson seems to convince most of the gang members, but not Joe, because he remains angry that she has lied to him about her own past and is now betraying him again. He drives everyone out of the store, but then, in the dark and alone, he recovers his feelings for Mary and decides to steal a bottle of perfume to make it up with her. As he walks by the cash register, he rethinks this act of theft, writes out a sales slip and puts the money for the perfume into the register, repeating the imagery of the musical number that began the movie. There is a close-up of his fingers pushing the keys on the cash register that may even be one of the shots used in the original number. We might say that when he is alone he realizes that he is not going to get the great reward of being part of a gang again, and so accepts Mary's logic.

When he gets home, however, he finds that she has gone; he then needs to use his "mob" buddies to find her, which results in a smaller montage sequence of searching for her. The gang members end up using their old criminal skills: for example, in the caper, Gimpy was a lookout on a street corner; in the search for Mary, Gimpy is seen again being a kind of lookout as he searches for her. The movie ends when the whole gang assembles at the maternity ward; Joe carries his bottle of perfume in to her, and Gimpy carries the baby Mary has just delivered . So the movie ends with the complete revision of the gang into a support for the private family. Mathematical logic seems to triumph over crowd emotion. Or, to be more precise, mathematical logic supported by the emotional thrills of consumerism: the perfume Joe brings Mary is named "hour of ecstasy," so in a sense it is bottled emotional pleasure, bottled orgasm, which provides an emotional force to replace the pleasure of mob unity.

Mary functions in this movie as Katherine does in *Fury*: both women teach their men that love is better than the emotions which tie gangs together. We can see how much Lang has rejected his earlier logic if we contrast these women to the role of Maria in *Metropolis*: her love is won only when Freder learns to be one with the workers, when he has experienced himself as a cog in the overall system—in other words, when he has joined the gang. Only by accepting a public role and giving up his private "garden" can he win the love that satisfies his desires. The ideal love in *Metropolis* mirrors and joins with the emotions felt at a mass gathering; the ideal love in *Fury* and *You and Me* replaces those public emotions with "hours of ecstasy" brought from the social order into private life.

In *Fury* and *You and Me*, Lang proposes ways to tame the powerful mass emotions that create mob behavior and threaten to tear the social order apart. His most well-known Hollywood movie, *The Big Heat*, is about trying to create powerful mass emotions in order to destroy the dictatorial gang structure that is corrupting a city. The movie moves toward the moment of riot—the moment when "the big heat" will appear—but in this case the riot will be an uprising of "citizens" against the rule of the mob. The head of the criminal gang, Mike Lagana, says quite directly that he is afraid of what will happen if the public gets "hot" enough: "We've stirred up enough headlines. The election is too close. Things are changing in this country, a man who can't see that hasn't got eyes. Never get the people steamed up—they start doing things, grand juries, election investigations, deportation proceedings. I don't want to end up in the same ditch with the Lucky Lucianos." The notion that the public would throw out the mob if they were "heated" enough turns the logic of Lang's German movies to the support of individualism. And what seals this logic is that what provides the lever to crack open the mob and release to the public the emotions which will bring the "big heat" are the emotions unleashed by the breaking up of private relationships. Actually, the only real crimes we see this mob perpetrate are acts of attacking women in order to stop possible leaks. The mob destroys private lives in order to preserve the collective, the gang. But in this movie, each act of destruction of a private relationship has the effect of transforming what was previously sexual into emotions of anger and revenge, directed at the mob.

The central such act is actually a mistake: the mobsters seek to kill a detective, Bannion, who is investigating them, but their car bomb accidentally kills his wife instead. This killing becomes the emotional motivation that drives him to eventually crack the mob, and in a sense his entire effort is an attempt to restore private life. His method of investigation is to insinuate himself into the private life of the most vicious mobster, Vince Stone, a fellow who enjoys hitting women. Bannion befriends Stone's girlfriend, Debbie, and she eventually follows Bannion to his hotel room, where it seems she wishes to seduce him. He, however, ends up telling her about his wife: the movie suggests then that what is attractive about Bannion is that he offers what private life can be. Bannion inserts into the private lives of the mobsters an image of what private life should be (we might say he gives Debbie a Hollywood movie vision).

Bannion also discovers that another woman, Bertha Duncan, is blackmailing the mob with information her husband provided before he committed suicide. Bannion comes very close to killing her in order to release that information because then, as he puts it, "the big heat follows." But

Bannion of course cannot commit a crime even if the result would be to break up the bigger crimes of the whole mob. Instead, the movie sets it up so that Debbie, the mob woman who has gained from Bannion the vision of ideal private life, kills Bertha to unleash the big heat. She does so after her lover, Stone, in anger at her having visited Bannion, throws boiling water in her face. As Debbie puts it to Stone after she commits the murder, "Bertha Duncan is dead . . . The lid is off the garbage can and I did it."

What will folllow the big heat is presumably something akin to what follows Lincoln's "heating" up the audience at the trial in *Young Mr. Lincoln*—the aroused public will take proper action to arrest the real criminals, those who are violating private life. That it requires a murder to bring about this restoration of morality is a quandary that appears often in Hollywood movies. I suggest that part of the problem is that the movies cannot believe in the power of facts alone: it requires a kind of passion, even a criminal passion, to alter the crowd emotions that maintain criminal gangs.

In many Lang movies, the necessity of passion to overcome passion means that the operation of movies are set against themselves: undoing the distortions of morality created by crowd emotion requires a distortion of morality by some individual under the influence of powerful emotions. In order to let the truth be seen, someone has to use distortions of truth. And this problem applies to the truth that movies present as well. Hollywood movies have to transcend what seems "true" as presented within movies in order to reveal "truth": something has to transcend "movie reality" as a regular part of Hollywood movies, because movie reality is precisely that which creates false mass consciousness, whether or not the scenes it represents are "true."

Fury repeatedly undermines what appears simply "true" and represented in the most well-lit and easily readable scenes. Joe's death is only one such moment that turns out not to be so easily readable: the crimes committed by the townspeople, revealed in the perfectly clear, well-lit movie footage taken by a journalist within this movie, have to be reinterpreted after Joe's confession, so that their convictions are overturned by evidence of his manipulation. What he manipulated was the meaning of that footage: the images seemed to mean that the townspeople were murderers, but when Joe is not dead, the images just show them to be rather reckless rioters. Similarly, in *You Only Live Once*, the close-up of the hat with Eddie's name on it has to be undermined by the discovery of the real killers. And even after these corrections have been made, we cannot simply rest assured that now we are seeing "the truth": the ends of these movies present, as the locus of final truth, scenes that transcend photographic realism. In *Fury*, Joe finally breaks out of his vicious desire for revenge when he—and we in the audience—hear Katherine's voice while he looks once again at the bedroom scene in the store window which began the film. He turns and realizes it is just his imagination. Soon after that, we see along with him the hallucination of the faces of the townspeople who will die if he persists, and we hear march music pursuing him as he runs down a shadow-filled street to escape those faces. It requires these moments of distortion of reality to bring Joe to restore truth. Similarly, in *The Big Heat*, it is only when Debbie has been physically distorted by the boiling water that her emotions become powerful enough to commit murder, a distortion of morality that has the effect of bringing on the big heat that will restore morality to the whole city.

We are left at the end of these movies with the sense that the only answer to the distortions created by crowd emotions is other distortions which create contrary emotions. Lang's movies suggest then that nobody is ever free of crowd emotions. The glib assurance that the Hays Code provides that moviemakers can control the "suggestions" that are inserted by movies into audiences' minds depends on the assumption that moviemakers themselves are free of distorting crowd emotions.

Returning to Germany

Lang was troubled all his life by the sense that he could not control the "moral suggestions" made by his films, because he was confronted repeatedly by critics who declared that his early movies contributed to the rise of Nazism.[9] Lang aggressively countered such claims. During World War II, he made several overtly anti-Nazi films, even collaborating with Berthold Brecht on one, and he claimed repeatedly that he had always been against the Nazis. He circulated a dramatic story of his last-minute escape from Germany after Goebbels tried to enlist him as head of the national film production effort (a story that many years later was proven false). He even claimed that he had surreptitiously put Hitler's words in the mouth of the arch-criminal Mabuse in the last film he made in Germany as an act of resistance just before he left the country. His anti-Nazi American films and his dramatic stories never succeeded in exculpating his German films, for one very simple reason: his very close collaborator on all his German films, his wife Thea Von Harbou, was an active supportor of the Nazi Party while working with him, and, after he emigrated, she stayed in Germany, joined the Party and made movies for the Nazi government during World War II. If Lang wanted his later anti-Nazi movies to provide the basis for judging the politics of his early movies, wouldn't the later pro-Nazi movies which Von Harbou made undermine any such claims? How could Von Harbou, the screenwriter and pro-Nazi, have put words from Hitler into the mouth of the twisted, ugly criminal Mabuse, as Lang claimed? Was her pro-Nazi sentiment so much less powerful than his anti-Nazi sentiment that their films should be seen as basically his?

Lang's desire in the 1940s to prove that he had been an anti-Nazi even before they came to power was in part a reaction to what the Nazis were doing with his early films. Some were actively promoted, and one was even incorporated into Nazi propaganda. In 1940, the Nazis made an anti-Semitic "documentary," *The Eternal Jew*, in which they used a clip from what has become known as Lang's and Von Harbou's greatest masterpiece, *M*. The new propaganda film uses the confession of the child-killer Hans Beckert in *M* as a representation of a Jew making fraudulent excuses for his evil acts. The 1940 propaganda film implies that *M* is not just the story of a strange maniacal killer but also a work revealing the diseased mentality of the Jews, and so a call for a group like the Nazis to come to power.

Lang's inability to convincingly demonstrate that he had not been a proto-Nazi filmmaker led to a very unusual final phase to his career: after Von Harbou died, he returned to Germany and made two more films. One was a two-part remake of a film on which he and Von Harbou had been screenwriters in 1921; the other was a sequel to the last movie the two of them made before Lang left Germany in 1931. In other words, he made revisions of precisely the very first movie and the very last movie on which he and Von Harbou had worked together. While re-making these two films, he said he felt a "circle beginning to close."[10] The phrase suggests that he saw in these last films a way to bend together the two halves of his career, to make his life into one overall circle rather than two disjointed lines. These movies became for him the capstones of his career: after them, he never completed another film, though he lived for sixteen more years, moved back to Hollywood and was offered numerous projects. Something about those last two films ended his sense of what he could do as a filmmaker.

What he seemed to be trying to do in those last two films was to show that he could still produce movies like his earliest ones, and at the same time prove that those early films were not really proto-Nazi films. He could not simply deny that there was any relation between his German work and Nazism, so what he did instead was create what are essentially allegorical "explanations" of how he could have been himself an anti-Nazi and yet have made films which ended up seeming to serve the Nazi cause. Both the movies tell stories of how a man can get caught up in corrupt political plots without having political goals, and the method is the classic Hollywood formula: the heroes fall in love with women who are inextricably entwined with corrupt political systems, so that the heroes have to become involved with politics in order to save the woman. Such an explanation of course fit his life exceptionally well: he could claim to have been seduced by his love for Von Harbou into making proto-Nazi films without knowing it. And of course in these movies the man ends up rescuing the woman and at the same time saving the nation from the bad politicians. It is not hard then to see these movies as allegorically being fantasies of rescuing Von Harbou and the movies they made together, as well as rescuing Germany from having succumbed to Nazism.

The key feature that suggests that the corrupt politicians in these movies are screens for Nazis is that the politicians are trying to stir up mass riots to overthrow the current regime and install themselves as dictators. But the methods the evil characters in these movies use are straight from Hollywood: they seek to manipulate women into certain marriages, which, it turns out, would serve to foment those riots. In other words, these movies provide the ultimate Hollywood "explanation" of regimes such as Nazism, which seem to emerge from the passions of crowds: those passions are actually just distorted versions of sexuality and love.

Let me explain how this works in the two movies: in the two-part thriller, known as *The Indian Tomb* (though the first segment was released as *The Tiger of Eshnapur*), the central problem is that a dancer is being held captive by the maharajah of Eshnapur to force her to love him. A German engineer meets the dancer while she is traveling, falls in love with her, and, eventually, rescues her from the maharajah. Entwined with this love story is a secondary plot of an evil competitor, Prince Ramigani, half-brother to the maharajah, who believes that if the maharajah marries the dancer, the people will riot because the dancer is not of royal blood, and that riot will put Ramigani into power. To produce this result, Ramigani captures the German engineer and threatens to kill him unless the dancer says she will marry the maharajah. The engineer escapes his captivity, rescues the dancer, and in effect leads the maharajah's army against

Ramigani. I suggest that this subplot of a regime threatened with a corrupt ruler as a result of public riots is a subtle allusion to the rise of Nazism.

The allusion to Nazism may seem rather a stretch in this movie, but it is much clearer in the movie Lang went on to make after *The Indian Tomb*. This movie, the last he ever made, also has the same double structure, in which the rescue of a woman from a bad marriage at the same time saves a regime from public riots which could lead to a dictator, but in this movie the person plotting to become a dictator is directly identified as seeking to continue the goals and methods of Nazis after the end of World War II—and is also directly identified as continuing the actions of a central figure from the early films of Lang and Von Harbou. In that last movie, *The Thousand Eyes of Dr. Mabuse*, the man seeking dictatorial power, Dr. Jordan, pretends to be Dr. Mabuse, a supercriminal from two of Lang and Von Harbou's 1930s movies. Mabuse had nearly magical mental powers; Dr. Jordan has some hypnotic power but manages to appear supernatural by using leftover Nazi technology, in the form of a hotel which the Nazis filled with hidden cameras. The Nazis built this hotel to spy on world figures who visited Germany; Jordan uses it to masquerade as a clairvoyant and to gain power over various rich persons in pursuit of the same goal the Nazis sought—world dictatorship.

The hero of this movie is an American, Henry Travers, who is in Germany on business after World War II. The main plot of this movie is Dr. Jordan's manipulation of a love affair: he tricks Travers into falling in love with a young woman, Marion Menil, in hopes that Travers would marry her and then be killed so that Marion would inherit Travers's resources for Jordan to use—particularly a nuclear rocket, which Jordan plans to set off to create mass chaos. But Dr. Jordan's plan fails because Marion really falls in love with Travers, which breaks Jordan's hypnotic control over her. In Lang's last two movies then, an outsider comes into a country to save a woman from a bad marriage and simultaneously saves the country from riots that would lead to an evil dictatorship. The mass chaos planned by evil leaders to gain power in these two movies never happens, and as such they function rather wistfully as revisionist history—as if some hero had stopped Hitler before he came to power.[11]

But more important to our understanding of Lang's effort to undo the "collectivist" or Nazi "suggestions" in his early films is to note which elements Lang revised. A key feature which Lang removed in remaking his early films is the figure of a "superman"—the mythic heroes and almost magical criminals who can inspire mass crowd reactions of either worship or fear. Nazism fed on the fascination with and fear of such figures. In Lang's remakes, Lang reduces the religious and magical power of such figures, making them into much more ordinary persons: not only the heroes, but the villains become "Joe Does." In the 1921 version of *The Indian Tomb*, there is a man with divine powers, a yogi named Ramigani; he is forced to work for the maharajah by a mystical requirement that once awakened from his meditative underground sleep he has to grant the wishes of whoever wakens him. While he provides the mystical powers that the maharajah needs, the yogi clearly is presented as morally rejecting everything the maharajah wants to do, and also as predicting that the maharajah's plans will end in disaster. In the 1958 remake, there is no mystical yogi Ramigani, but instead the name has been transferred to the maharajah's half-brother, a man trying to gain power though military force and murderous threats. The yogi in the early film is a figure of great fascination and potentially the moral center of the movie—and as such, could be seen as contributing to the fascination with powerful supernatural figures which slips toward Nazism. In the remake, Ramigani has no great personal charisma, no magical powers; he is simply an evil man with an army. So the moral ambivalence and mythic power of the original Ramigani is removed.

Lang's last movie revises the figure from the early Weimar movies with the most direct political agenda and the most magical powers over public opinion: Dr. Mabuse. Mabuse died in the earlier movies, but his writings eerily resurrected him by taking possession of the body of other men who read them. In the postwar movie, Dr. Jordan borrows the aura of Mabuse by hiding behind a curtain, claiming to be Mabuse, and carrying out the plans Mabuse left behind. Dr. Jordan does have some hypnotic powers, but most of his seemingly magical power turns out to be due to his spying with the Nazi cameras and his manipulating his voice with recording equipment. This movie seeks to "demystify" the strange powers Mabuse had seemed to have, to reveal that what had seemed supernatural personal qualities can now be explained away as just the results of technology. Indeed, one could say that the movie credits the movies themselves with creating Mabuse's powerful hypnotic illusions.

This movie is thus a meditation on the hypnotic power of movies, and as such it reaches the disturbing conclusion that it really does not matter whether movies promote love or dictatorship: in either case they leave no room for individuals, because even the love affairs will end up being designed by others. Lang's last two movies focus quite intently on the ways that seemingly private love affairs can be manipulated or even created for political ends. In *The Indian Tomb*, Prince Ramigani tries to get the dancer to fall in love with the maharajah or at least to fake that love because Ramigani believes that such a love and the ensuing marriage would lead to regime change. He believes that a public image of love can serve as a significant political force; in a sense his plot is a version of what *Casablanca* proposes as well—having a woman go off with a public figure rather than with the man she truly loves because that public love affair will have powerful political repercussions. Ramigani fails to create the public image of love and the true lovers—the dancer and the engineer—escape to live happily ever after. The movie ends comfortably settled within the Hollywood fantasy.

The last movie is much more disturbing: in it, the good love affair that the movie makes us wish would triumph seems completely manufactured by the evil manipulator, Dr. Jordan, as part of his political plot. The movie does show that this love grows so strong that it breaks Dr. Jordan's control and wrecks his plans. But the lovers do not then live happily ever after: though the movie ends with the couple's last kiss, the woman has already been shot by Jordan and she dies as the kiss ends. In other words, the movie does not show the lovers actually being extricated from Jordan's plots: the end of those political plots is precisely the end of the love affair. The sad ending suggests that the love could not be separated from the fake plots which created it. Is this Lang's admission that he could never rescue his love affair with Von Harbou from her involvement with Nazis, because in some sense their love was a product of that involvement? The movie suggests that their collaboration was so successful—and their love so intense—only because they were tapping into large "plots" going on around them which fueled the emotions in their films and in their private lives. Lang and Von Harbou then both were caught up in the story of the rise of Nazism, and their love affair was partly a product of that larger story. We could say then that Lang fell into a movie already in progress when he fell in love.

The Thousand Eyes of Dr. Mabuse goes to great lengths to show precisely that when the hero Travers falls in love, he falls into a movie directed by someone else. Travers watches through a one-way mirror as Marion is abused by her awful husband, and when the husband finally threatens her with a gun, Travers bursts through the mirror, snatches up the gun and shoots the husband. It appears exactly as if Travers is breaking through the screen into a movie and changing its plot (figs. 26 and 27).

Later we discover that this entire scene was a fraud—the gun is a fake, the husband is a fake, the woman is not married to anyone, and Travers

Figs. 26–27. Watching life as a movie . . .

and breaking into the frame.

was set up to break through the mirror in order to get him to fall in love with the woman. The rescue of Marion from a vicious lover was in effect a Hollywood movie staged for Travers, and he falls for it and into it. When he jumps through the screen, he is then not disrupting a plot but just fulfilling his assigned role in a movie in progress. We even see that the "screen" he breaks though—the mirror—is just a stage prop in a larger movie because just after he breaks through the one-way mirror, the camera pulls back and we realize we have been watching everything on a TV screen, the screen from which Dr. Jordan, the man who thinks he is Mabuse, is directing this entire plot.

This movie has numerous lines in it about the sense that everything is under surveillance, subject to public display and control. For example, there is one exchange where Marion says to a policeman, "This is my personal life and none of your business," to which the cop answers, "When the police are involved, there is no personal life." It is precisely this interchange of dialogue that gets at the core of the issue that haunts Lang's last movies and turns them into a disturbing commentary on the two film styles and the two political systems I have been exploring. The Hollywood system implies that mass emotions can be harnessed to support "personal lives" and thereby preserve individuality, but this movie implies that the mass shaping of private lives—particularly as Hollywood does it—destroys individuality. The movie implies that private life is actually policed by the action of movie cameras. Further, this policing does not simply catch people who commit crimes; rather it operates by creating the scenery of private life in the first place.

Nothing in this movie escapes being caught up in a story being directed by someone else. The love between Mary and Henry, which supposedly breaks them free of Jordan's control, is created by Jordan's plot. Even Jordan himself, who would seem to be manipulating everyone else, is simply following Mabuse's script. If this movie is allegorically an effort to rescue Lang's love for Von Harbou and the movies they made together from her involvement with Nazism, then it ends up doing nearly the opposite: it suggests that their love was in effect created by the social forces and mysterious plots which swept Hitler into power. Lang and Von Harbou were caught up in a "movie" being written by history.

Critics who write about the politics of films cannot easily escape facing the same dilemma Lang faced when he sought to remake his movies: as critics write about films, we have to realize that, like Lang's characters, we are already "inside" other films being written by history. Lang's last two movies thus end up undermining a central presumption of both

144

criticism and the Hays Code: that it is possible to stand apart from the "suggestions" created by films, to recognize those suggestions and to act without being influenced by them. When Lang eliminated the supermen who, in his early movies, had the magical power to understand and shape mass emotions, he ended up eliminating his belief in the possibility of anyone's controlling the stories or texts or lives they try to create. Lang's own attempt to "close the circle," to give shape to his whole career by uniting his collectivist and his Hollywood styles, simply undermined both styles, by implying that when he tried to make films, they ended up making him. And he never made another movie.

NOTES

Introduction. Movies and the History of Crowd Psychology

1. Le Bon, *The Crowd*, xiv–xv.
2. Nye, *Origins of Crowd Psychology*, 170.
3. Quoted in Steven J. Ross, "Beyond the Screen: History, Class and the Movies," in *Hidden Foundation*, ed. James and Berg, 38
4. Ibid., 40.
5. The Motion Picture Producers and Distributors of America, "The Motion Picture Production Code of 1930," in *Movies in Our Midst*, ed. Mast, 323.
6. Ross, *Silent Film and the Shaping of Class*, 87.
7. The Motion Picture Producers, "The Motion Picture Production Code," 323.
8. Herbert Blumer, "Moulding of Mass Behavior Through the Motion Picture," *Publications of the American Sociological Society* 19 (1936): 123. Cited in Austin, *Immediate Seating*, 100.
9. Thomas Doherty, "This Is Where We Came In: The Audible Screen and the Voluble Audience of Early Sound Cinema," in *American Movie Audiences*, ed. Stokes and Maltby, 143.
10. Schwartz, *Spectacular Realities*, 179.
11. Brill, *Crowds, Power and Transformation in Cinema*; Canetti, *Crowds and Power*. For other theories of crowd psychology, see Le Bon, *The Crowd*, and Moscovici, *Age of the Crowd*. For a discussion of Le Bon's theories in relation to modernism, see Tratner, *Modernism and Mass Politics*.
12. Cavell, *World Viewed*, 35.
13. Kracauer, *Theory of Film*, 51.
14. Eisenstein, "Through Theater to Cinema," in *Film Form*, 16.
15. Marx and Engels, *Basic Writings*, 57.
16. Hitler, *Mein Kampf*, 478–79.

17. Gaines, *Fire and Desire*, 250.

18. Lippmann, *Principles of the Good Society*, 294–95.

19. Cited in Moscovici, *The Age of the Crowd*, 26.

20. Freud, *Group Psychology*, 94.

21. Ibid., 93.

22. Ibid., 93.

23. A movie's popularity is determined by its domestic gross. See Box Office Mojo, "All Time Box Office Adjusted for Ticket Price Inflation," at http://www.boxofficemojo.com/alltime/adjusted.htm (accessed August 11, 2004).

24. Cameron is quoted in Patrick McGee, "Terrible Beauties: Messianic Time and the Image of Social Redemption in James Cameron's *Titanic*," *Postmodern Culture: An Electronic Journal of Interdisciplinary Criticism* 10, no. 1 (1999), paragraph 31. http://muse.jhu.edu/journals/pmc/v010/10.1mcgee.html.

25. McPhail, *Myth of the Madding Crowd*.

Chapter 1. Collective Spectatorship

1. Doane, *Femmes Fatales*; Diawara, *Black American Cinema*.

2. Hansen, *Babel and Babylon*.

3. Margolis, *Cinema Ideal*, xiv.

4. Nick Browne, "The Spectator-in-the-Text: The Rhetoric of *Stagecoach*," in Braudy and Cohen, *Film Theory and Criticism*, 148–63.

5. Hansen, *Babel and Babylon*, 4.

6. The Motion Picture Producers, "The Motion Picture Production Code," 322–23.

7. Hansen, *Babel and Babylon*, 86.

8. The Motion Picture Producers, "The Motion Picture Production Code," 323.

9. Mill, *Utilitarianism*, 73.

10. Ibid., 73.

11. The Motion Picture Producers, "The Motion Picture Production Code," 323.

12. Ibid., 323.

13. Althusser, "Ideology and Ideological State Apparatuses," in *Lenin and Philosophy and Other Essays*, 170.

14. The Motion Picture Producers, "The Motion Picture Production Code," 323.

15. Stanley Cavell has analyzed the difference between an "actor" and a "star" in *The World Viewed*, 25–28.

16. Ibid., 321.

17. Dewey, *Individualism Old and New*, 82.

18. Ibid., 83.

19. Althusser, *For Marx*, 149–50.
20. Jarvie, *Movies and Society*, 89.
21. MacCabe, "Realism and the Cinema: Notes on Some Brechtian Theses," in *Tracking the Signifier*, 39.
22. Laura Mulvey, "Visual Pleasure and Narrative Cinema," in Braudy and Cohen, *Film Theory and Criticism*, 844.
23. MacCabe, *High Theory/Low Culture*, 4.
24. The editors of *Cahiers du Cinema*, "John Ford's *Young Mr. Lincoln*," in Nichols, *Movies and Methods*, 493–529.
25. Ibid., 517.

Chapter 2. Constructing Public Institutions

1. Mimi White similarly observes that "The major impact and significance of the film is shown to be the disruption of family units." See "*The Birth of a Nation*: History as Pretext," in Lang, *D. W. Griffith, Director*, 220.
2. Geduld, ed., *Focus on D. W. Griffith*, 99.
3. Dewey, *Individualism Old and New*, 82.
4. Miriam Hansen, "The Hieroglyph and the Whore: D. W. Griffith's *Intolerance*," in Gaines, *Classical Hollywood Narrative*, 179.
5. Brill, *Crowds, Power and Transformation in Cinema*, 38.
6. Hansen, "The Hieroglyph and the Whore," 197.

Chapter 3. The Passion of Mass Politics

1. The Movie Times maintains an updated list of the most popular movies of all time in constant dollars at http://www.the-movie-times.com/thrsdir/Top10everad.html. I am citing the list as presented August 14, 2002.
2. Cameron is quoted in McGee, "Terrible Beauties," 31st of 45 paragraphs (see intro., note 24). Other critics who argue that *Titanic* is based on Marxist themes include James Kendrick, "Marxist Overtones in Three Films by James Cameron," *Journal of Popular Film and Television* 27, no. 3 (1999): 41 and Peter N. Churno, "Learning to Make Each Day Count: Time in James Cameron's *Titanic*," *Journal of Popular Film and Television* 26, no. 4 (1999): 63.
3. Ray Merlock, "*Casablanca*, Popular Film of the Century," *Journal of Popular Film and Television* 27, no. 4 (2000), 2–4.
4. Rosemary Welsh, "Theorizing Medievalism: The Case of *Gone With the Wind*" in Utz, *Medievalism in the Modern World*, 314.
5. Richard King makes a similar point that "*Gone with the Wind* provides the literary account of the origins of the urban, commercial, and financial middle class that arose from the destruction of the prewar planter class" in Richard

King, "The 'Simple Story's' Ideology: *Gone with the Wind* and the New South Creed," in Pyron, *Recasting*, 170.

6. Louis Rubin Jr., "Scarlett O'Hara and the Two Quentin Compsons," in Pyron, *Recasting*, 89.

7. Hitler, *Mein Kampf*, 394.

8. There is a similar scene with a similar effect at the end of *The Grapes of Wrath*, as Tom Joad is about to disappear from his family because of political causes rather as Ilsa is about to disappear from Rick. Ma asks how she will know what happens to Tom when he leaves her. She sees their relationship being broken up by his involvement in mass politics. He answers, however, by proposing that they will remain connected by something bigger than their family, a mass soul:

> Like Casey said, a fellow ain't got a soul of his own, just a little piece of one big soul . . . then it don't matter, I'll be all around in the dark, everyone, wherever you can look; wherever there is a fight so hungry people can eat, I'll be there. I'll be in the way guys yell when they're mad; the way kids laugh when they're hungry and know supper's ready.

Tom's line is very much like Rick's, that individual people don't matter much in the face of something more important to the masses. What we see, however, in these Hollywood movies, as we hear about the mass soul or the world that dwarfs individual lives, are close-ups of stars; we feel intense desire for these stars to remain with us, not to leave, and this desire to be with the stars is the very emotion these movies rely on to make us desire involvement with political movements.

And just as Rick mentions Paris as what allows him to leave Ilsa—in other words, his love motivates his joining the mass anti-Nazi movement—so Tom ends up telling Ma to look for moments when a parent is feeding a child to understand where he is. In other words, in both movies the emotions of the private sphere—intimate familial love—are what carry people into the mass.

9. McGee, "Terrible Beauties," paragraph 43.

Chapter 4. Loving the Crowd

1. Marx and Engels, *Basic Writings*, 57.
2. Ibid., 63.
3. Hitler, *Mein Kampf*, 478–79.
4. Eisenstein, "A Dialectic Approach to Film Form," in *Film Form*, 57.
5. Ibid., 53.
6. Ibid., 62.
7. Ibid., 46.
8. Eisenstein, "Methods of Montage," in *Film Form*, 81.

9. Nichols, *Blurred Boundaries*, 126.

10. Eisenstein, "Through Theater to Cinema," in *Film Form*, 16.

11. Marx and Engels, *Basic Writings*, 247.

12. Laura Mulvey, "Visual Pleasure and Narrative Cinema," 834, and Peter Wollen, "Godard and Counter Cinema: *Vent D'Est*," in Braudy and Cohen, *Film Theory and Criticism*, 499.

13. Nichols, *Blurred Boundaries,* 112.

14. Ibid., 112–13.

15. Quoted in Margarita Tupstyn, "From the Politics of Montage to the Montage of Politics," in Teitelbaum and Freiman, *Montage and Modern Life*, 87

16. Ibid., 102.

17. Hayden White, "The Historical Text as Literary Artifact," in Leitch, *Norton Anthology of Theory and Criticism*, 1719.

18. Stuart Hall, "Cultural Studies and Its Theoretical Legacies," in Leitch, *Norton Anthology of Theory and Criticism*, 1901.

19. Marx and Engels, *Basic Writings*, 247.

20. Berman, *Modern Culture*, 102.

21. Quoted in Miriam Hansen, "America, Paris, the Alps: Kracauer (and Benjamin) on Cinema and Modernity," in Charney and Schwartz, *Cinema and the Invention of Modern Life*, 387.

22. Hitler, *Mein Kampf*, 448.

23. Ibid., 297.

24. Ibid.

25. Ibid., 301.

26. Ibid., 303.

27. Ibid., 449.

28. Kaja Silverman, "[On Suture]" in Braudy and Cohen, *Film Theory and Criticism*, 140.

29. Ibid.

30. Hitler, *Mein Kampf*, 478–79.

31. Quoted in Berman, *Modern Culture*, 101, 106.

32. Cited in Berman, *Modern Culture*, 110.

33. Marcuse, "State and Individual Under National Socialism," in *Technology, War and Fascism*, 84.

34. Terri J. Gordon, "Fascism and the Female Form: Performance Art in the Third Reich," in Herzog, *Sexuality and German Fascism*, 177.

35. Ibid., 198.

36. Nichols, *Blurred Boundaries*, 33.

Chapter 5. From Love of the State to the State of Love

1. Gunning, *Films of Fritz Lang*, xii.

2. Quoted in Gunning, *Films of Fritz Lang*, 219.

3. Bordwell, Staiger, and Thompson, *Classical Hollywood Cinema*, 82.

4. Peter Dolgenos, "The star on C. A. Rotwang's door: Turning Kracauer on its head (an analysis of Fritz Lang's film, the '*Metropolis*')," *Journal of Popular Film and Television* 25, no. 2 (1997): 68–75; John Tulloch, "Genetic Structuralism and the Cinema: A Look at Fritz Lang's *Metropolis*," *Australian Journal of Screen Theory* no.1 (1976): 3–50.

5. Gunning, *Films of Fritz Lang*, 198.

6. Ibid., 197.

7. McGilligan, *Fritz Lang*, 223.

8. Wilson, "Fritz Lang's *You Only Live Once*," in *Narration in Light*, 33–48; Gunning, *Films of Fritz Lang*, 243–45.

9. Most of the directors who came from Europe were accused of selling out, though they actually brought numerous innovations to Hollywood, as James Morrison has ably demonstrated in *Passport to Hollywood*.

10. Quoted in Bogdanovich, *Fritz Lang in America*, 111.

11. Gunning, *Films of Fritz Lang*, 460, describes the final Mabuse movie as completing a kind of history of twentieth-century Germany: the final antebellum Mabuse movie, *The Last Testament*, "marked . . . Germany on the verge of a Nazi takeover"; the postwar Mabuse movie marked "Germany's survival of both the Third Reich and defeat in World War II." Gunning concludes that in Lang's films, "The spectre of Mabuse, the persistence of his criminal legacy . . . brood over a trilogy that embraced the history of Germany in the twentieth century."

SELECTED BIBLIOGRAPHY

Austin, Bruce A. *Immediate Seating: A Look at Movie Audiences*. Belmont, Calif.: Wadsworth, 1989.

Alexander, William. *Film on the Left: American Documentary Film from 1931 to 1942*. Princeton, N.J.: Princeton University Press, 1981.

Althusser, Louis. *For Marx*. Translated by Ben Brewster. New York: Pantheon Books, 1969.

————. *Lenin and Philosophy and Other Essays*. New York: Monthly Review Press, 1971.

Belton, John, ed. *Movies and Mass Culture*. New Brunswick, N.J.: Rutgers University Press, 1996.

Benjamin, Walter. *Reflections: Essays, Aphorisms and Autobiographical Writings*. Edited by Peter Demetz. Translated by Edmund Jephcott. New York: Schocken Books, 1978.

Berman, Russell A. *Modern Culture and Critical Theory: Art, Politics and the Legacy of the Frankfurt School*. Madison: University of Wisconsin Press, 1989.

Bogdanovich, Peter. *Fritz Lang in America*. London: Studio Vista, 1967.

Bordwell, David. *The Cinema of Eisenstein*. Cambridge, Mass.: Harvard University Press, 1993.

————. *Narration in the Fiction Film*. Madison: University of Wisconsin Press, 1985.

Bordwell, David, Janet Staiger, and Kristin Thompson. *The Classical Hollywood Cinema: Film Style and Mode of Production to 1960*. New York: Columbia University Press, 1985.

Braudy, Leo and Marshall Cohen, eds. *Film Theory and Criticism: Introductory Readings*. 5th ed. New York: Oxford University Press, 1999.

Brecht, Berthold. *Brecht on Theatre: The Development of an Aesthetic*. New York: Hill and Wang, 1964.

SELECTED BIBLIOGRAPHY

Brill, Lesley. "Canetti and Hitchcock, *Crowds and Power* and *North By Northwest.*" *Arizona Quarterly: A Journal of American Literatures, Culture, and Theory* no. 56 (2000): 119–46.

———. *Crowds, Power and Transformation in Cinema.* Detroit: Wayne State University Press, 2006.

Browne, Nick, ed. *Cahiers du Cinéma: 1969–1972: The Politics of Representation.* Cambridge, Mass.: Harvard University Press, 1990.

Burgoyne, Robert. *Film Nation: Hollywood Looks at U.S. History.* Minneapolis: University of Minnesota Press, 1997.

Butsch, Richard. *The Making of American Audiences: From Stage to Television, 1750–1990.* Cambridge: Cambridge University Press, 2000.

Canetti, Elias. *Crowds and Power.* Translated by Carol Stewart. New York: Viking, 1962.

Cavell, Stanley. *The World Viewed: Reflections on the Ontology of Film.* New York: Viking, 1971.

Charney, Leo and Vanessa R. Schwartz, eds. *Cinema and the Invention of Modern Life.* Berkeley: University of California Press, 1995.

Cook, David. *A History of Narrative Film.* 3rd ed. New York: Norton, 1996.

Davies, Philip and Brian Neve, eds. *Cinema, Politics and Society in America.* New York: St. Martin's Press, 1981.

Debord, Guy. *Comments on the Society of the Spectacle.* Translated by Malcolm Imrie. London: Verso, 1990.

———. *Society of the Spectacle.* Detroit: Black and Red, 1983.

Deleuze, Gilles and Felix Guattari. *Anti-Oedipus: Capitalism and Schizophrenia.* Translated by Robert Hurley, Mark Seem, and Helen R. Lane. Minneapolis: University of Minnesota Press, 1983.

Desser, David and Garth S. Jowett, eds. *Hollywood Goes Shopping.* Minneapolis: University of Minnesota Press, 2000.

Devereux, Leslie and Roger Hillman, eds. *Fields of Vision: Essays in Film Studies, Visual Anthropology, and Photography.* Berkeley: University of California Press, 1995.

Dewey, John. *Individualism Old and New.* New York: Minton, Balch, 1930.

———. *Liberalism and Social Action: The Page-Barbour Lectures.* New York: G. P. Putnam's Sons, 1935.

Diawara, Manthia, ed. *Black American Cinema: Aesthetics and Spectatorship.* New York: Routledge, 1993.

Doane, Mary Anne. *Femmes Fatales: Feminism, Film Theory, Psychoanalysis.* New York: Routledge, 1991

Dyer, Richard. *Stars.* New ed. with a supplementary chapter by Paul McDonald. London: British Film Institute, 1998.

Eagle, Herbert. *Russian Formalist Film Theory.* Ann Arbor: University of Michigan Press, 1981.

Eisenstein, Sergei. *Film Essays and a Lecture.* Edited by Jay Leyda. New York: Praeger Publishers, 1970.

————. *Film Form: Essays in Film Theory.* Translated by Jay Leyda. New York: Harcourt Brace Jovanovich, 1949.

————. *The Film Sense.* Translated by Jay Leyda. New York: Harcourt Brace Jovanovich, 1975.

————. *Nonindifferent Nature.* Translated by Herbert Marshall. Cambridge: Cambridge University Press, 1987.

Freud, Sigmund. *Group Psychology and the Analysis of the Ego.* Translated by James Strachey. New York: Bantam Books, 1965.

Gabler, Neal. *Life: The Movie: How Entertainment Conquered Reality.* New York: Vintage, 2000.

Gaines, Jane, ed. *Classical Hollywood Narrative: The Paradigm Wars.* Durham, N.C.: Duke University Press, 1992.

————. *Fire and Desire: Mixed-Race Movies in the Silent Era.* Chicago: University of Chicago Press, 2001.

Geduld, Harry M., ed. *Focus on D. W. Griffith.* New York: Prentice-Hall, 1971.

Goodwin, James. *Eisenstein, Cinema, and History.* Urbana: University of Illinois Press, 1993.

Gunning, Tom. *The Films of Fritz Lang: Allegories of Vision and Modernity.* London: British Film Institute, 2000.

Hansen, Miriam. *Babel and Babylon: Spectatorship in Silent Film.* Cambridge, Mass.: Harvard University Press, 1991.

Heath, Stephen and Patricia Mellencamp, eds *Cinema and Language.* Los Angeles: The American Film Institute, 1983.

Heath, Stephen. *Questions of Cinema.* Bloomington: Indiana University Press, 1981.

Herzog, Dagmar, ed. *Sexuality and German Fascism.* New York: Berghahn Books, 2005.

Hitler, Adolf. *Mein Kampf.* Translated by Ralph Mannheim. New York: Houghton Mifflin, 1971.

hooks, bell. *reel to real: race, sex, and class at the movies.* New York: Routledge, 1996.

Iampolski, Mikhail. *The Memory of Tiresias: Intertextuality and Film.* Translated by Harsha Ram. Berkeley: University of California Press, 1998.

James, David E. and Rick Berg, eds. *The Hidden Foundation: Cinema and the Question of Class.* Minneapolis: University of Minnesota Press, 1996.

Jameson, Fredric. *The Political Unconscious: Narrative as a Socially Symbolic Act.* Ithaca, N.Y.: Cornell University Press, 1981.

————. *Signatures of the Visible.* New York: Routledge, 1990

Jarvie, I. C. *Movies as Social Criticism.* Metuchen, N.J.: Scarecrow Press, 1978.

————. *Movies and Society.* New York: Basic Books, 1970.

Kaes, Anton, Martin Jay and Edward Dimendberg, eds. *The Weimar Republic Sourcebook.* Berkeley: University of California Press, 1994.

Kittler, Friedrich A. *Gramophone, Film, Typewriter.* Translated by Geoffrey Winthrop-Young and Michael Wutz. Stanford, Calif.: Stanford University Press, 1999.

Kracauer, Siegfried. *Theory of Film: The Redemption of Physical Reality.* New York: Oxford University Press, 1960.

Lang, Robert, ed. The Birth of a Nation*: D. W. Griffith, Director.* New Brunswick, N.J.: Rutgers University Press, 1994.

Le Bon, Gustave. *The Crowd: A Study of the Popular Mind.* 2nd ed. New York: Macmillan, 1897.

Leitch, Vincent B., ed. *The Norton Anthology of Theory and Criticism.* New York: Norton, 2001.

Lippmann, Walter. *An Inquiry into the Principles of the Good Society.* Boston: Little, Brown, 1947.

———. *The Phantom Public.* New York: Harcourt, Brace, 1925.

———. *Public Opinion.* New York: Harcourt, Brace, 1922.

Lukács, Georg. *Essays on Realism.* Edited by Rodney Livingstone. Translated by David Fernbach. Cambridge, Mass.: MIT Press, 1980.

MacCabe, Colin. *Tracking the Signifier: Theoretical Essays: Film, Linguistics, Literature.* Minneapolis: University of Minnesota Press, 1985.

MacCabe, Colin, ed. *High Theory/Low Culture: Analyzing Popular Television and Film.* New York: St. Martin's Press, 1986.

Marcuse, Herbert. *Technology, War and Fascism.* Vol. 1, *Collected Papers of Herbert Marcuse.* Edited by Douglas Kellner. London: Routledge, 1998.

Margolis, Harriet E. *The Cinema Ideal: An Introduction to Psychoanalytic Studies of the Film Spectator.* New York: Garland, 1988.

Marx, Karl and Friedrich Engels. *Basic Writings on Politics and Philosophy.* Edited by Lewis S. Feuer. New York: Anchor Books, 1959.

Marris, Paul and Sue Thornham. *Media Studies: A Reader.* 2nd ed. New York: New York University Press, 2000.

Mast, Gerald, ed. *The Movies in Our Midst: Documents in the Cultural History of Film in America.* Chicago: The University of Chicago Press, 1982.

May, Larry. *The Big Tomorrow: Hollywood and the Politics of the American Way.* Chicago: The University of Chicago Press, 2000.

McArthur, Colin. *Dialectic: Left Film Criticism from* Tribune. London: Key Texts, 1971–78, 1982.

McCann, Richard Dyer. *Film and Society.* New York: Scribner's, 1964.

McClelland, J. S. *The Crowd and the Mob: From Plato to Canetti.* London: Unwin Hyman, 1989.

McGilligan, Patrick. *Fritz Lang: The Nature of the Beast.* New York: St. Martin's Press, 1997.

McPhail, Clark. *The Myth of the Madding Crowd.* New York: Albert de Gruyter, 1991.

Messaris, Paul. *Visual Literacy: Image, Mind and Reality.* Boulder, Colo.: Westview Press, 1994.

Metz, Christian. *Film Language: A Semiotics of the Cinema.* Translated by Michael Taylor. New York: Oxford University Press, 1974.

———. *The Imaginary Signifier: Psychoanalysis and the Cinema.* Translated by Annwyl Williams. Bloomington: Indiana University Press, 1986.

Mill, John Stuart. *Utilitarianism, On Liberty, and Considerations on Representative Government.* Edited by H. B. Acton. London: Dent & Sons, 1972.

Monaco, Paul. *Cinema and Society: France and Germany During the Twenties.* New York: Elsevier, 1976.

Morrison, James. *Passport to Hollywood: Hollywood Films, European Directors.* Albany: State University of New York Press, 1998.

Moscovici, Serge. *The Age of the Crowd: A Historical Treatise on Mass Psychology.* New York: Cambridge University Press, 1985.

Nichols, Bill. *Blurred Boundaries: Questions of Meaning in Contemporary Culture.* Bloomington: Indiana University Press, 1994.

———. *Ideology and the Image: Social Representation in the Cinema and Other Media.* Bloomington: Indiana University Press, 1981

Nichols, Bill, ed. *Movies and Methods: An Anthology.* Berkeley: University of California Press, 1976.

Nye, Robert A. *The Origins of Crowd Psychology: Gustave Le Bon and the Crisis of Mass Democracy in the Third Republic.* London: Sage Publications, 1975.

Perez, Gilberto. *The Material Ghost: Films and Their Medium.* Baltimore: Johns Hopkins University Press, 1998.

Polan, Dana. *Power and Paranoia: History, Narrative and the American Cinema, 1940–1950.* New York: Columbia University Press, 1986.

Pyron, Darden Ashbury, ed. *Recasting:* Gone with the Wind *in American Culture.* Miami: Florida International University Press, 1983.

Reimer, Robert C. *Cultural History through a National Socialist Lens: Essays on the Cinema of the Third Reich.* Rochester, N.Y.: Camden House, 2000.

Rentschler, Eric. *The Ministry of Illusion: Nazi Cinema and its Afterlife.* Cambridge, Mass.: Harvard University Press, 1996.

Richter, Hans. *The Struggle for the Film.* Edited by Jürgen Römhild. Translated by Ben Brewster. New York: St. Martin's Press, 1986.

Roffman, Peter and Jim Purdy. *The Hollywood Social Problem Film: Madness, Despair, and Politics from the Depression to the Fifties.* Bloomington: Indiana University Press, 1981.

Ross, Steven J. *Silent Film and the Shaping of Class in America.* Princeton, N.J.: Princeton University Press, 1998.

Schnitzer, Luda, Jean Martin and Marcel Martin, eds. *Cinema in Revolution: The Heroic Era of the Soviet Film.* Translated by David Robinson. New York: Hill and Wang, 1973.

Schulte-Sasse, Linda. *Entertaining the Third Reich: Illusions of Wholeness in Nazi Cinema.* Durham, N.C.: Duke University Press, 1996.

Schwartz, Vanessa. *Spectacular Realities: Early Mass Culture and Fin-de-Siècle Paris.* Berkeley: University of California Press, 1998.

SELECTED BIBLIOGRAPHY

Sennett, Richard. *The Fall of Public Man*. New York: Knopf, 1977.

Silverman, Kaja. *The Subject of Semiotics*. New York: Oxford University Press, 1983.

Sloan, Kay. *The Loud Silents: Origins of the Social Problem Film*. Urbana: University of Illinois Press, 1988.

Stokes, Melvyn and Richard Maltby, eds. *American Movie Audiences: From the Turn of the Century to the Early Sound Era*. London: British Film Institute, 1999.

Strick, Philip. "The mob (the representation of crowds in films)." *Sight and Sound* 3, no. 5 (1993): 35–37.

Teitelbaum, Matthew and Lisa Freiman, eds. *Montage and Modern Life: 1919–1942*. Cambridge, Mass.: MIT Press, 1992.

Tratner, Michael. *Modernism and Mass Politics: Joyce, Woolf, Eliot, Yeats*. Stanford, Calif.: Stanford University Press, 1995.

Tudor, Andrew. *Image and Influence: Studies in the Sociology of Film*. New York: St. Martin's Press, 1975.

Utz, Richard and Tom Shippey. *Medievalism in the Modern World: Essays in Honour of Leslie J. Workman*. Turnhout: Brepols Publishers, 1998.

Vasey, Ruth. *The World According to Hollywood, 1918–1939*. Madison: The University of Wisconsin Press, 1997.

Vertov, Dziga. *Kino-Eye: The Writings of Dziga Vertov*. Edited by Annette Michelson. Translated by Kevin O'Brien. Berkeley: University of California Press, 1984.

Von Harbou, Thea. *Metropolis*. Intro. Forrest A. Ackerman. Rockville, Md.: James A. Rock & Company, 2002.

Welch, David. *Propaganda and the German Cinema*. Oxford: Oxford University Press, 1983.

Wilson, George M. *Narration in Light: Studies in Cinematic Point of View*. Baltimore: Johns Hopkins University Press, 1986.

INDEX

INDEX

Hays Code: as basis of theory of collective
 spectatorship, 12–21, 25–31; con-
 trasted to norms of collectivist films,
 65, 74; and Fritz Lang, 112, 117,
 131, 137, 145; and Hollywood's
 fear of masses, 3–9, 57
Hitler, Adolph, 6, 8, 10, 62, 65, 74; Fritz
 Lang and, 113, 118, 138–40, 144;
 in Riefenstahl's films, 91–96, 102,
 105, 108
HUAC, 3

identification, collective, 21–23, 60–62,
 91, 95–96, 101
Indian Tomb, The, 139–42
Intolerance, 45–50

JFK, 76
Jarvie, I. C., 22
Jews, 71, 91, 105, 111, 118, 125, 138
Junger, Ernst, 97–98

Kracauer, Siegfried, 6, 91, 125
Ku Klux Klan, 33–35, 40–45, 108

Lacanian theory, 23–25
Lang, Fritz, 10, 24, 109–45
Le Bon, Gustav, 1–2
Lenin, Vladmir, 76
light: as image of a divine source of the
 state, 99–107; as representation of
 movie projection, 27–31, 104, 115,
 118
Lippmann, Walter, 9
long shot, 17, 37–38, 52–54, 60, 78, 82,
 101
Love Story, 72
lynch mob, 26–29, 42, 126–27

M, 110–11, 118–26, 138
MacCabe, Colin, 23–24
machines. See technology
male gaze, the, 2; Eisenstein's modification
 of, 79–80, 85; Riefenstahl's modification of, 95–105
Man with a Movie Camera, The, 85–90, 93
Marcuse, Herbert, 98
Marx, Karl, 6–8, 74–78, 88–89

Marxist theories, 9, 22–24, 51, 70, 90–91
mass resistance to suggestion, 5–7, 15–16,
 74, 112
mass suggestion, 13, 30, 96
McGee, Patrick, 68
Merlock, Ray, 51
Metropolis, 110–18, 132–34
Metz, Christian, 2
Mill, John Stuart, 15–19, 91
monarchy, 34–35, 96
money, 63, 68, 71–72, 105–6, 127–34
montage, 54, 98, 113–14, 129–34; Eisenstein's theory of, 74–76
monumental figures, 31, 91–97, 107–8
Morris, Errol, 76
mountains: as image of nature outside the
 state 57, 60; as image of the state,
 45–48, 52, 104–7
Movie Production Code of 1930. See Hays
 Code
Mulvey, Laura, 2, 23, 78

Nazi Party, the 6, 18, 73–74; in Hollywood movies, 52, 57, 60–66;
 Lang's relation to, 10, 24, 109, 118,
 125, 137–45; Riefenstahl's relation
 to, 90–108
Nichols, Bill, 76, 83, 85

October, 75
Olympia, 92–99, 104, 107

projection, movie: images of, 27–29, 65,
 86–87, 99–105, 111, 115; theory
 of, 13–14
psychoanalytic psychology, 10–13, 17, 24–
 28, 51–53

race, 9, 18, 33–44, 50–51, 59–63, 91,
 105–7
Rand, Ayn, 19
realism: fascist version of, 95–98; in Hollywood movies, 28–31, 34, 43,
 131–37; montage as alternative to,
 74–76, 85–90; in spectator theory,
 15–17

160